Third Edition

90+ DAYS OF PROMOTING YOUR BOOK ONLINE

Your Book's Daily Marketing Plan

PLUS
"After 90 Days!"

Day-by-Day Promotional Tasks for Ongoing Sales

Angela Hoy

and

Richard Hoy

BookLocker.com

WritersWeekly.com

AbuzzPress.com

BoostABook.com

Library of Congress Control Number: 2011914099

Library of Congress Cataloguing-in-Publication Data
Hoy, Angela J. 1967-
Hoy, Richard D., 1967-
90+ Days of Promoting Your Book Online: Your Book's Daily
Marketing Plan / Angela Hoy, Richard Hoy
ISBN 978-1-60145-460-7
  1. Authorship—Marketing. 2. Books—Marketing. 3. Selling—
     Books.

Printed on acid-free paper.

BookLocker.com, Inc.
2020

Third Edition

DISCLAIMER

This book details the authors' personal experiences with and opinions about book promotion.

The authors and publisher are providing this book and its contents on an "as is" basis, and make no representations or warranties of any kind with respect to this book or its contents. The authors and publisher disclaim all such representations and warranties, including for example warranties of merchantability and advice for a particular purpose. In addition, the author and publisher do not represent or warrant that the information accessible via this book is accurate, complete, or current.

Please consult with your own legal, accounting, or other licensed professional regarding the suggestions and recommendations made in this book.

Except as specifically stated in this book, neither the authors nor publisher, nor any authors, contributors, or other representatives will be liable for damages arising out of or in connection with the use of this book. This is a comprehensive limitation of liability that applies to all damages of any kind, including (without limitation) compensatory; direct, indirect or consequential damages; loss of data, income or profit; loss of or damage to property and claims of third parties.

You understand that this book is not intended as a substitute for consultation with a licensed professional. Before you initiate any change to writing or publishing business, you will consult with a licensed professional to ensure that you are doing what's best for your situation.

This book provides content related to book promotion topics. As such, use of this book implies your acceptance of this disclaimer.

Dedication

Dedicated to our amazing BookLocker.com family of authors.

Table of Contents

INTRODUCTION

Glory day! Your new book is finally published! You're excited that your baby has hit the streets (or the Internet) and you can't wait to start pounding that virtual pavement, and collecting the royalties. I know what you're thinking. You're an author, not a marketer. Not to worry. We have more than two decades of online book selling experience under our belts and we're going to teach you how to promote your book effectively online. And, almost all of our techniques are FREE!

WHAT'S THE BIGGEST MISTAKE AUTHORS MAKE?

If you really want to sell books, don't do what most authors do - dump your book at a few websites and walk away, hoping it'll catch on some day. That just doesn't happen today. Promoting your book online should be considered at least a part-time job. Highly successful authors spend more time promoting a book than they do writing it—a *lot* more.

Online book promotion is not only simple but, if you have a step-by-step, day-to-day marketing plan (this book!), it can also be a very artistic endeavor, which makes it fun for creative folks like authors (you!).

Here are some little-known, depressing factoids about the traditional publishing industry:

Traditional publishers use the profits from low- to mid-selling books to promote their best sellers. Many publish books by unknown authors, and then do nothing more than send out a couple dozen review copies in the hopes that one or two books by those unknowns might catch the eye of the public and the media.

Even if you are lucky enough or talented enough to land a traditional contract, if your name isn't as well known as Stephen King or Tom Clancy, you will be responsible for the majority, if not all, of the marketing activities for your book.

If you come up with some marketing ideas that were not offered in your contract, like a unique book tour, magazine ads, etc., you'll have to pay for them out of your own pocket.

If you ask your publisher to help you pay for those items, they'll probably refuse to do so. If you wanted them to help pay for your book promotion, you should have gotten that in writing in your contract. Problem is, troublesome new and unknown authors who demand those perks up front usually don't get traditional publishing contracts. Why should the publisher offer to pay money they know *you* are eventually going to spend for them later out of sheer desperation for sales?

None of the marketing activities you conduct and pay for when promoting your traditionally published book will entitle you to one penny more of the profits that you're already giving your traditional publisher (around 88%–94% for them vs. 6%–12% for you).

Okay, now that we have the depressing part over with, let's move on.

The book you're reading right now is Angela's 12th non-fiction title. She has written books for freelance writers and authors, for mothers wanting to attempt a vaginal birth after having a prior cesarean, for women who are facing an imminent divorce, a how-to craft book on reborning dolls (which has done *very* well on eBay, by the way—more on that later), and more. In the '90s, she published one of the very first electronic books (ebooks)—before "ebook" was a household word—and long before Stephen King ever thought of it. She simply started selling the MSWord file of one of her books online, and it was instantly successful. Why? 1. It was available for immediate delivery; 2. It was less expensive than the print version, and; 3. The customer didn't have to pay shipping. After spending so much time having booklets printed up at Kinko's, creating mailing labels, stuffing large envelopes, and taking daily trips to the post office, we sure wish we'd thought of selling books as electronic files sooner!

Angela then wrote the ebook *How to Write, Publish & Sell Ebooks,* which brought in more than $700 in sales on the first day she put it on her website! Nowadays, the more books she writes, the more money she makes. When you write multiple books targeting the same audience, you can expend the same amount of marketing effort as you would for one book, but you naturally sell more books. The more successful authors are those who promote multiple titles to the same audience. Yes, it really is that simple.

I know this is starting to sound like we're on the pep-squad so we'll stop. We just want you to know that we know what we're talking about and what we do isn't that difficult, or even expensive, despite what some people and companies would like you to believe. Those people and companies are the ones selling high-priced marketing products and services for authors...and often coercing authors into spending more money than they will ever make on any resulting book sales. The tips in this book can lead to far more book sales than spending hundreds or thousands of dollars on promotional coffee mugs, book fairs, or expensive magazine or newspaper ads.

Think about it. If you paid someone to publish your book, your publisher is profiting from book sales. So, why would they charge an author thousands of dollars for a marketing product or service designed to sell books? If a fee-based publishing company had complete confidence in a product or service designed to sell their own books, wouldn't they be giving it away free? They don't and here's why. They know they're going to make far more money from authors paying for those services than they will from any resulting book sales. And, they know their authors are not going to make a profit from those expensive services, either.

For the purposes of this book, we're assuming you, like us, have a real job and that you don't have eight hours a day to spend promoting your own book. Some of the daily tasks might take an hour or less but others will take longer. We suggest setting aside a specific period of time each day to do the steps in this book. Angela's best time for writing and marketing is the first hour or two of each morning, depending on her planned tasks for that day. That enables her to accomplish her priorities before the rest of the day railroads her down different paths (like answering email, formatting books for other authors, homeschooling our youngest child, etc.).

There are also "ongoing" marketing tasks that are noted in some chapters with this symbol: +

Those ongoing tasks are summarized near the end of this book (see "AFTER 90 DAYS: YOUR BOOK'S DAILY MARKETING PLAN"). Those marketing activities can and should be conducted on a continuing basis. So, if you do everything this book recommends, you'll be promoting your book far longer than just 90 days.

Let's get started, shall we?

PART I

90+ Days of Promoting
Your Book Online

IMPORTANT NOTE

When you see a + next to any specific day in the book, it indicates an ongoing marketing activity, one that you'll need to perform repeatedly while you continue to promote your book. Please refer to the chapter titled "AFTER 90 DAYS: YOUR BOOK'S DAILY MARKETING PLAN" for a recommend schedule of these ongoing marketing activities.

Before Day 1:

You <u>MUST</u> Have a Website that <u>YOU</u> Control

If you already have your own website, you might be tempted to skip to the next chapter. Please don't because there are a few nuggets below.

If your book was traditionally published, you need to have your own website where you can publish your own writing, feature your own marketing content, correspond with readers, collect email addresses for your newsletter or blog, and more. Do not allow your publisher to be responsible for, or in any way whatsoever have control over *your* website. You should direct all potential readers to *your* website first, *not* your publisher's.

If your book is self-published, it is imperative that you not fall for the "author's website" your publisher may try to sell you. You must have a website with your own website address ("URL" or Uniform Resource Locator) that *you* own and control. It doesn't matter whether your website is only one page or several. You must have one. We don't care how great your publisher makes their "book page," or "author page," or "author website" or whatever they call it sound. You must own your own website outright, and have current and future control over the pages to which you are referring all future buyers in all your press and marketing efforts. Why? Here's an example:

Andy Author published his book with a self-publishing company. Sure, he'd read lots of bad comments about the company online but they were one of the biggest so, really, what could go wrong? He paid them over $1,500 to publish his book, and then let them talk him into buying one of their "author websites" for another few hundred, plus a $30 monthly website hosting fee.

Andy was an effective self-promoting author. Once his book was published, he participated in online interviews, radio shows, and even landed a couple of local television appearances. He started to get noticed and people were buying his book. Because of his marketing prowess, literally hundreds of websites mentioned his publisher's "Author Website" address. Unfortunately, he started hearing from readers that they were receiving books with upside-down pages, broken binding, and more. The complaints were starting to hurt Andy's reputation, and reviewers were even mentioning the poor quality of his books in their book reviews. Furthermore, he didn't believe his publisher was reporting all the sales of his book, nor paying all the royalties due.

Andy's book was good but his publisher was not. He had to get out. He terminated his contract, and hired a publisher with a better reputation to produce his book. The problem was that people were still seeing his old publisher's "Author Website" address (URL) in all that press he'd generated over the previous months. And, guess what the publisher had done with that URL? They were redirecting it to another book, written by another author! Poor Andy checked his contract and discovered that, despite that he'd paid them to create that "Author Website," they did indeed own and have complete control over it. All his past online marketing efforts were now making money for another author...and his old publisher.

Even if Andy had landed a traditional contract, and parted on good terms with the self-publishing company, or even if he'd terminated his contract because they had defaulted on the contract for any reason at all, he'd still have lost complete control over the "Author Website" that he paid for!

What Andy should have done from the very beginning was purchase his own URL, something like AuthorAndySmith.com. (We suggest authors try to purchase their name if they can so they aren't limited on the topics of their future books. For example, Angela owns AngelaHoy.com. See more hints about names in Richard's section, which follows.) Had Andy purchased his own domain name, and referred everyone to that URL when performing his marketing tasks, he could have simply changed the link for the "buy me" button on his own website to the new publisher's page, or to Amazon.com, or to

BarnesandNoble.com, or to wherever he chose to send his readers on any particular day.

If you don't have your own website, get one now. You can pick out your own domain, and get a website at a very reasonable rate using the site https://wordpress.com (more about this later in the chapter). You could even have your own website up and running by the end of the day. As soon as you do, add some content, and start using that domain name in all your marketing efforts. You can then simply put a "buy me" button on your new website, and direct that link to your book's page on your publisher's site, or to a specific online bookstore, or wherever else you want. And, you can change that "buy" link anytime you want, especially if you change publishers someday, if one store in particular is running a promotion, if you want to start selling the book yourself, or even if you land a traditional contract in the future.

What about those free websites or those nifty free blogging sites? If another company owns the URL, you not only don't have control over it but that company could terminate your "site" for any reason, and could even go out of business, among other things. Imagine spending months or years creating content on a site that just vanishes one day. So, again, buy and manage your *own* URL.

There are lots of books on the market about how to create a website. But remember, you don't need a huge website with multiple pages, graphics, and lots of (annoying) bells and whistles. You really just need a few marketing pages, and most importantly, control over the "buy me" link!

WARNING: When I landed a traditional contract with a co-author years ago, we purchased a domain name that complemented the title of the book. Richard then started building the website while we waited for the book to hit the market. Later, the publisher told us we needed to turn that website over to them. Yeah, right! That was *not* part of the original contract and the website belonged to *us*. We believe the traditional publisher knew we were going to be sending potential readers to our own website instead of theirs and they wanted future control of the site where buyers were going to buy the books. We're also certain other traditional publishers have tried to claim ownership of individual author websites over the years, too, so be careful! If it's not in your contract, they can't take it away from you. If you are offered a contract that demands control over your website, either don't sign the contract at all, or make sure they delete that clause before you agree to sign.

If your book is traditionally published, you need to be wary of what your publisher might try to do to sabotage your personal marketing efforts for their own gain. For example, they may make more money selling your book directly to readers than they do when you purchase copies at your author discount. Your own website, no matter what it's called, is *your* property and they have no right to claim ownership of it just because you sold them the rights to your book. Of course, you should always read your contract in its entirety, and have your agent and/or attorney review it as well to ensure that no such website ownership or other ridiculous clauses exist.

So, what exactly should you include on your website, and what domain name should you choose?

What Am I Going to Put on My Website?

by Richard Hoy

For authors, the website really serves as a way to build a readership to which they can later pitch their books, and future books. So, how do you build a readership? Essentially, you want to create content people want to read, and you want them to come back on a regular basis. The easiest way to do this is to *create your own online publication*.

In later chapters, we'll go into exactly how you develop content people want to read. But, for now, it's important that you set up a website with the proper infrastructure to handle all the things you need to become a successful online publication.

It is easy to get overwhelmed with all the details of setting up a website. A successful site, though, needs to have at least these two capabilities:

1. A way to display both static information (the content that stays the same over time, like your contact information) and changing/updated information (the articles people read).

2. A way to inform readers of updated information (when you post new articles) so they will come back on your timetable.

Rather than go on about the countless options, we recommend a simple, inexpensive website from https://wordpress.com.

The First Step: The Domain Name

Let's take a step back from the website for a moment, and talk about choosing a domain name, the address of your website. Many people new to website ownership pick domain names off the cuff, but that's not the best way to go about it.

You want your domain name to have these qualities:

1. It should be easy to say.

Imagine how saying these website addresses in an interview, over the phone, or even in person can result in confusion:

www.doubleyou.com
www.dotdot.com
www.dotcom.com

2. It should be easy to spell.

Don't use words in a name that people commonly misspell like: "accessories" or "conscientious."

3.) It should not be confusing:

ExpertsExchange.com >> ExpertSexChange.com
TherapistFinder.com >> TheRapistFinder.com
PotsOfArt.com >> PotsoFart.com

Avoid Having the Domain You Want Taken Out From Under You

If you've ever searched for a domain name to buy on a website that sells them, this might have happened to you.

You go to a website that sells domains and do a search to see what's available, but decide to wait, and think about it for a day. When you come back the next day, you discover the domain has been taken by someone else. This is not a coincidence. It is called Domain Name Front Running. The details of how this works are beyond the scope of this book. If you want to know more, search for "domain name front running" in your favorite search engine.

The bottom line, though, is you should be ready to buy the domain name when you search for it on a site that sells domain names.

An easy way to see whether a domain is taken that will help protect you from getting scammed by frontrunners is to type the domain name you want into your web browser, and see whether a website comes up. If a site does come up, the domain is not available. If you get an error message, there is a good chance the domain is still available (though it could still be taken).

Using this method, you can develop a list of your top three to five picks for a domain name.

Stick to domain names that end in ".com." That is the form most people recognize. Also, if a .com name is taken and you choose .net instead, you run the risk of a trademark infringement lawsuit (and the loss of your website) later. You must choose your own original name that nobody else has ever used. Google any name or phrase you're considering to see whether anyone else has a company, product, or service by that name. You can also search for trademarked names and phrases at http://tmsearch.uspto.gov.

Buying a Website from <u>Wordpress.com</u>

There are lots of options when buying website services. However, in our opinion, the most bang-for-your-buck is a software platform called Wordpress.

Originally, WordPress entered the scene as free blogging software. Because it had to be installed on a web server to work, it was, for many years, something only computer nerds would use.

A few years back, the creators of WordPress realized that most people are not, in fact, computer nerds, and developed Wordpress.com - a website hosting service for the rest of us based on the WordPress software.

As with any service trying to make a buck, WordPress offers many bells and whistles you can buy à la carte. But, one nice thing they do offer is a bundle of services to get you started. You can see their offerings here:

<u>https://wordpress.com/pricing</u>

Public Versus Private Domain Registration

When WordPress asks you to create an account, which they use as the official contact information associated with the domain, whatever you put in these blanks will be accessible to the public unless you pay an extra fee to keep it private. If you have an address and phone number you don't mind making public, use it at this point to create the account. Otherwise, you'll have an option to select the "private registration service."

IMPORTANT: We do NOT recommend making your physical address public. No matter how obscure your book, or how small the potential audience, there is always the chance that some overzealous fan or reader might want, shall we say, face-to-face contact with you. This has happened to Angela on occasion and some contacts have been downright scary. We strongly recommend you provide only a P.O. Box if you choose to make your address public.

WordPress has a detailed explanation of public versus private domain registration here:

https://wordpress.com/support/domains/domain-registrations-and-privacy/

Days 1–3:

Unique Content = A Successful Website

by Richard Hoy

If you already had your own website when you bought this book, you may have skipped to this chapter. Although you probably already have content on your website, please read this chapter because it contains advice all authors should follow.

In the online world, "content" refers to the material you put on your website to attract visitors.

Websites that have regular readers have two features in common:

1. The content is unique
2. The content is updated regularly

Both features make sense. Why would anyone visit a site that has basically the same content as any other site? And, why would they visit more than once if the content never changes (excluding, of course, sites that are reference material)?

Some of you may have one or more books on the same topic and others may have books on multiple topics. For the latter, you can create different sections on your website for each topic/genre. For this exercise, we're going to assume you are creating new pages on your website that will promote one of your books.

Where Do You Start?

The first step is to understand the type of website visitor you want to attract. You can do that by answering these questions:

1. Who is my target audience?

2. What makes my book unique?

We'll use a real example. Let's say your book is about bonsai trees, which is "the art of growing dwarfed, ornamentally shaped trees or shrubs in small shallow pots or trays." (Thanks, Dictionary.com.)

That means the answer to question number one is "People interested in growing bonsai trees."

Let's say your book has specific chapters on using unusual species to create bonsai trees, like maple trees or lemon trees. It's those chapters that make your book different from other bonsai tree books on the market, and that answers question number two.

You can use these two insights as the basis for the content of your website.

We should take a step back here, and point out that search engines (the primary way people find new websites) love unique content. That's why it's so important. Therefore, the object here is to figure out what content you can put up that will make your site stand out from the rest in the search engines, yet still attract enough readers to make your efforts worthwhile.

Remember, niche is better. So instead of writing about "bonsai tree care" write about "olive bonsai trees," or some other niche in the bonsai category. There may be fewer people searching on that term, but that also means there is less competition from other websites, increasing the chances that your article will be found first. Plus, recall that we identified above the niche that makes the book in our example unique—it has chapters on using unusual species to create bonsai trees—so other phrases from the list like "bonsai grape tree," "bonsai orange tree," and "lemon bonsai tree" would also make great content for your site.

A great free tool for doing keyword research is https://AnswerThePublic.com, which uses autosuggest data to build lists of phrases people are actually entering into the search engines Google and Bing:

You can also enter the phrase "Keyword Research Tool" in your favorite search engine to come up with other services and options for performing this research.

NOTE: See Day 12 for a more in-depth discussion on keywords.

___ Day 1

Using the instructions above, develop a keyword or phrase list around which you can write unique articles for your website.

___ Days 2–3 +

Using one of the keywords / phrases from your search yesterday, write a unique article, edit it, and publish it on your website.

+ This is an ongoing activity. Please refer to "AFTER 90 DAYS: YOUR BOOK'S DAILY MARKETING PLAN" near the end of this book.

IMPORTANT: **You should load your website early with at least five unique articles.** Try to write and edit at least one per day this week. You should aim to add a new article to your site once per week thereafter. The more unique content you feature, the more popular your website will be (and the more books you'll sell). Unique content also makes your website more attractive to search engines.

Days 4–11:

The Absolute <u>BEST</u> Online Book Promotion Tool!

Your Ezine/Newsletter or Blog!!

by Angela Hoy

You MUST Reach Out to Readers,

Not Wait for Them to Remember You Exist!

I've always said that the best way to sell a book online is to publish an ezine (a.k.a. an electronic newsletter). Why pay someone to advertise repeatedly in *their* publication when you can create your *own*? Offer quality editorial on a regular basis (weekly, bi-weekly, monthly—the more frequent, the better), and reach out to your readers via an ezine. Should you blog instead? Sure, but only if you email your readers each time you post an update. Blogs use special software that makes adding and updating content extremely easy, but you can use that software to publish your ezine as well.

Ezine or Blog?

If you create a typical blog, you'll have to wait for people to come back to visit you (but only after they remember you exist) or you'll have to hope they have an RSS feed (most people don't). It's never a good idea to try to convince people to start using new software just to read your material. The easier you make it for them, the more subscribers you will get. Pretty much everybody has an email address so sending out an ezine once a week or so via email will reach far more people than blog updates that aren't announced by email…or anywhere at all.

If you publish an ezine or a blog, you can collect your potential readers' email addresses (with their permission, of course), and connect with them on your schedule (again, only if they've agreed to receive emails from you). You don't have to wait for them to remember to come back to visit because you're reminding them about updates to your ezine, your website and, most importantly, your book(s) on a regular basis via email.

At WritersWeekly.com, we use a blog format to publish our ezine along with an abbreviated email issue that drives traffic (our subscribers) to the website each week. The email issue features teasers that direct readers to our website for the full articles. So, we have the ease of posting and publishing on the website's blog format, along with the ongoing readership of an ezine.

If you choose to publish a blog, much of the information in this chapter will apply to you anyway, so keep reading.

If your book is non-fiction, you can easily create quality, free editorial content on a regular basis. If your book is fiction, you get to have lots of creative fun.

Most of my books are written for writers. Our online publication, WritersWeekly.com, is an example of a successful ezine that uses blogging software. We give away free editorial each week in the form of an email featuring links to the current website issue, which includes paying jobs for freelance writers and editors, paying magazine market listings for writers, feature articles, marketing secrets for writers and authors, titillating industry news, and much more. At the same time that we are informing and entertaining our readers, we are also promoting my writing-related books, writing-related books by other authors, and our successful publishing company, BookLocker.com.

Years ago, WritersWeekly (under a different name) was distributed monthly. When we switched from monthly to weekly, our sales quadrupled. I still kick myself for waiting so long to figure that out!

If your book is fiction, consider offering either quality editorial (get creative!) or entertainment for your readers through your ezine. Here are some very basic ideas on what you can offer readers on a regular basis for specific fiction genres:

Historical fiction—Real stories or factoids about that period in history for history buffs like yourself; a discussion list on which readers can swap stories or information

Romance—Romantic ideas for men and women; reviews or discussions about romance products; a romance advice column; romantic stories submitted by readers

SF/Aliens—Timely coverage of UFO sightings across the globe, critical analysis of those sightings; a page where people can report their own UFO experiences to you for publication on your website

Religious Fiction—Weekly affirmations or inspirational messages; religious news; inspirational stories submitted by readers

Other—Consider having your main character (or other characters) converse with your readers through your ezine/blog; post your main character's diary entries online, and allow readers to comment; post fictional "news stories" about the characters in your book

Here's a brief primer on profitable email publishing:

First, the obvious. Name your ezine. Take your time on this step. The name of your ezine is as important as the name of your website and the titles of your books. Our ezine has the same name as our website.

Next, don't waste time reinventing the wheel. Research competitors (and others), and emulate how they format their ezine issues, both online and via email. Text ezines are still popular but many people create HTML issues now.

Create different sections for your first issue. Two or three are fine to start. You can always change, add, or delete some later, according to your readers' comments and requests. Create a generic, sample issue to send out to new subscribers in the interim. People love instant gratification!

Once you've created a sample issue, you are ready to start collecting the email addresses of your potential fans. When I first launched

WritersWeekly, I kept my list of subscribers in a simple spreadsheet, and used my email program's blind carbon copy (BCC) option when sending out each weekly issue. Later, it got too big and we had to switch to a professional list and mailing service. You can start soliciting email addresses on your website via a form, or you can simply ask website visitors to email you. A form is preferred, however, because spam filters are making doing business by email increasingly ineffective and frustrating. Most large Internet Service Providers (ISPs) use hard filtering to kill suspicious emails even before they arrive in the recipient's own spam folder. You don't have to do anything naughty to get blacklisted. Your email can be hard filtered simply based on a word appearing in it, or the ISP you use, or even because some spammer used your email address at one time to send out junk. Many companies and individuals have lost business due to undelivered emails.

Some authors don't have the technological know-how to create web forms. Per the previous chapter, WordPress can help to a certain extent. If you've opted for a professional website that is hosted by a web design firm, they can absolutely help. You also have the option of hiring someone to enhance your website. Just remember to not give anyone else complete control over your website!

One woman we know had her boyfriend set up her website. He did it under his own name and, when they broke up a years later, he took her website with him. She lost everything, including several years' worth of original articles. Never let anyone else have complete control over YOUR intellectual property.

One way to entice readers to subscribe to your ezine is to offer something free. I offer a choice of two free ebooks to new subscribers at WritersWeekly.com. This has been very effective over the years. If you're a fiction author, you can offer a long article as a free ebook, or perhaps something readers don't get in your book (maybe copies of letters written by the main characters, or pages from the main character's diary?). Get creative. You can think of something your readers might be interested in getting as a bonus for subscribing.

One thing is certain. If you don't offer a free bonus to potential new subscribers, you're going to have a very hard time building a good subscriber list. People don't like to give out their email address unless they have a very good reason to do so. A free product, even if it's electronic, is a great temptation.

In large, bold letters on your homepage, post a teaser about the newsletter/ezine and urge readers to subscribe, and get their free ebook or other product "TODAY!"

When someone subscribes, send them the current issue of your ezine, and add them to your list of subscribers so they'll receive future issues. Whenever somebody unsubscribes from your publication, immediately remove their email address from your list. Spam accusations can ruin a reputation.

As I wrote above, I initially kept our subscribers in a spreadsheet, and used my mail program's BCC function to send out each issue. We now have it entirely automated. Once your list grows a bit, and if you feel you need mailing list software ideas, type "mailing list software" or "email list software" into your favorite search engine. Wordpress has apps for this and your web hosting service likely has options available as well.

Don't stop at creating email issues. You need to post the content from each new issue to your website as well. Because this is new content, it makes your website more attractive to search engines and, the bigger your website, the more material you have that people on search engines might be looking for. In addition, readers who don't get your email issue because of spam filters can go to your website each week if they want to see the current issue. To see how we do it, go to WritersWeekly.com and click around a bit. You can see the teasers, and click on those for the actual articles.

And for heaven's sake, start promoting your ezine and free ebook via your email signature! Most email programs have an automated signature option. See Days 21–23 for more information.

___ Day 4

Name your new ezine

Get a sample issue of WritersWeekly.com

Make a list of ideas for sections to include in your ezine

___ Days 5, 6

Create your first issue

___ Day 7

Post your first issue on your website, format it for email delivery (refer to the WritersWeekly example for help, or use design templates from WordPress, of from your website hosting company), and make it available to email to new subscribers immediately on request, either manually or via an automated system.

___ Day 8

Create a free ebook or other informational/entertaining product to give away to new subscribers.

___ Day 9

Create a way for people to submit their email addresses to you, and for you to manage those email addresses (either manually by email, or via an automated web form on your website). Put that information on your website. This may tie in to your mailing list software or WordPress app if you choose to purchase or download that. Research and create a way to manage your subscribers and distribute the email issues at the same time. Again, when I first began, I kept a simple spreadsheet of my subscribers. It was easy and free.

___ Day 10

Post a large ad on your homepage inviting people to subscribe to your ezine or newsletter, and to receive your free ebook or other free product. This appears on the top, left-hand corner of every page of our website:

Home   SUBSCRIBE (IT'S FREE!) AND GET A FREE BOOK!

And, this pop-up appears when people first visit the site, or if they haven't visited in awhile:

Add a blurb about your newsletter (and the free goodie) to your email signature, and also to the signature you use when posting to websites, discussion groups, mailing lists, or blogs online. Be subtle so you aren't accused of spamming. More about responsible online posting appears in future chapters.

___ Day 11

Make a schedule. Plan to distribute a new issue by email *and* post it to your website on a regular basis (the more frequent, the better). Create plenty of ads promoting your book(s) for your ezine and website, and start adding those on a periodic basis, trying each one on a different week to see which one(s) generate more subscribers and, thus, sell more books.

Whatever you do, never *ever* add someone to your email subscriber list who hasn't specifically requested it. If you do, you will be reported as a spammer, get flamed to kingdom come, and your reputation will be tarnished. You could even lose your website hosting service or email address.

Okay, maybe that's more than eight days' worth of work. My mantra has always been *Better Too Much Than Not Enough*. (But I'm usually referring to chocolate or pizza when I say that.)

Day 12:

Finding the Keywords Your Potential Readers Are Really Using Online

by Richard Hoy

Keywords are topic-specific descriptions (single words and phrases) that generate the results people see when they use a search box on a website. Keywords and phrases are among the most vital tools you will use in your online marketing activities. You must be certain you are using the right ones.

Do you think you're using the best keywords and phrases for your book in your marketing efforts? You might be surprised to learn that the majority of people who may be interested in a book like yours might be using different keywords.

There are several nifty online tools that can help you find the most common search terms on your book's topic.

Here's an example:

These are the top marketing phrases Angela originally came up with for her VBAC book:

vbac
vaginal birth after cesarean
c-section
cesarean section
repeat cesarean section

Angela was pretty surprised to learn that, when I plugged her main keyword, VBAC, into the site, this is what popped up:

Count   Search Term
90,500   after c section

49,500	vbac
33,100	vaginal birth
22,200	after cesarean
8,100	vaginal birth after
4,400	after cesarean section
2,900	after a cesarean
720	vbac success

When I typed her number two choice, vaginal birth after cesarean, into the site, a whole other list of keywords and phrases appeared, none of which were on her list.

The number before each phrase is the number of times that phrase was searched on during the previous month.

For your book, focus on the niche topics. For example, entering "vbac" in Google.com yields about 1.5 million results. There's very little chance Angela's website/book excerpt/ezine will come up near the top of the search results just using that term. There's just way too much competition.

However, the phrase "vbac success" has far fewer results on Google.com. She stands a much better chance of coming up in the search results with content on that specific phrase. The gears in your head should be turning at this point. Ask yourself: What words or phrases should I really be using on my website, in my ezine or blog, on the web pages that describe my book, and in my other online marketing activities?

___ DAY 12

Go to this keyword research tool:

http://www.wordtracker.com

Enter a word or phrase and see what related keywords come up.

After doing what I did above, and determining your own most effective keywords and phrases, add them to your website's metadata, and save them for your Book Marketing Cheat Sheet, which is covered in the next chapter.

NOTE: You can also enter the phrase "Keyword Research Tool" in your favorite search engine to come up with other services and options for performing this research.

For help with keywords, phrases, and specific categories to use on Amazon, see:
https://marketplace.writersweekly.com/boost-a-book

Days 13–20:

Your Book Marketing Cheat Sheet

You will need several different text-based items when promoting your book online. To avoid jumping all over your computer looking for this, that, or the other, it's a good idea to create a Book Marketing Cheat Sheet for each of your books. Your Book Marketing Cheat Sheet should be a text-only document with no fancy formatting. This will prevent you from creating unnecessary symbols when copying and pasting into other websites.

Here is the information you should include in your Book Marketing Cheat Sheet:

___ Day 13

Create a new text file (your Book Marketing Cheat Sheet). And, please save often when doing this activity!

Different websites have different limits on the amount of content you can post. You're going to need three descriptions of your book, all at varying lengths. Write and then edit a Long Description of your book (up to 500 words). Add it to your Book Marketing Cheat Sheet.

___ Day 14

Re-read your 500-word description from yesterday with fresh eyes. Make any necessary changes, and do a final edit.

You'll now need to use that long description to create a shorter one. Copy and paste another copy of your 500-word description onto a new page in your Book Marketing Cheat Sheet. Start cutting that down (editing) to:

Create a Medium Description of your book (up to 300 words).

Once you're finished with that, edit it one last time, and then copy and paste another copy of your 300-word description onto a new page in your Book Marketing Cheat Sheet File. Just like above, start cutting that down (editing) to:

Create a Short Description of your book (up to 150 words).

Create a blurb (a very short description of less than 20 words)

Edit all of these one last time to ensure they are perfect.

Author Comment

An Author Comment (this is what Amazon.com calls it) is a personal message, in first person, from you, the author, to the potential reader concerning your book. We usually use a short version of the introduction of a book for this, provided it doesn't exceed 250 words.

___ Day 15

Write and edit your Author Comment (up to 250 words), and add it to your Book Marketing Cheat Sheet.

Author Bios

Many sites allow authors to post their biographies on pages where their book is featured. Although some, like Amazon, allow you to write quite a bit, others only allow a very short post.

___ Day 16

Write and edit a Long Author Bio (up to 500 words).

Write and edit a Short Author Bio (one short paragraph).

Add these to your Book Marketing Cheat Sheet:
Table of Contents and Back Cover Text

Many sites also allow authors to post their table of contents and back cover text online.

___ Day 17

If your book has a Table of Contents, copy and paste it into your Book Marketing Cheat Sheet...but remember to remove the page numbers because it will look silly if you include those on other websites.

Add the back cover text from your book to your Book Marketing Cheat Sheet.

Keywords

Please refer back to the previous chapter before completing this section.

If you were using a search engine to look for a book like yours, what keywords would you type in? You'll need different sets of keywords for posting to different websites online, as well as for your own marketing activities when searching for places online that might be able to help you promote your book.

Need some help? Who are your major competitors? What keywords are they using on their own websites or in their online bookstore pages? To find this information, go to the web page in question, right click on your mouse, and click View Source or View Page Source. You may need to click a bit to find the Source option in your browser. The text on that website will pop up in a window in HTML. You might need to put on your reading glasses but, if they're using keywords, you'll be able to find them in that information.

___ Day 18

Make a Primary, Short List of Keywords (up to 5 words/phrases) that are the ones you believe people will use most when searching for a book like yours.

Make a Secondary List of Keywords (10 additional words/phrases).

Make a Third List of Keywords (10 more words/phrases).

Add all of these to your Book Marketing Cheat Sheet.

Excerpts from Book Reviews/Comments

Unless you have obtained written permission from the author of a book review, you can't post/publish their review in its entirety anywhere. You need to obtain written permission from the actual reviewer and/or from the website or publication where that review appears, depending on who owns the copyright to the review. Although many reviewers are happy to allow authors this courtesy, some are working for publications. Those companies might own the rights to the book reviews they pay writers to produce.

Under Fair Use Copyright Law, you can quote briefly from copyrighted material, provided you cite the source.

You will probably receive fan mail from readers. When you receive a nice comment (even from family and friends who have read your book), thank the reader, and ask whether you can quote them in your marketing materials. The vast majority will be happy to let you do so but you should offer them the option of only using their first initial and last name, their first name and last initial, or just simply initials in the event they desire anonymity.

___ Day 19

Add two sections to your Marketing Cheat Sheet: Book Reviews and Reader Comments. Start pasting these review excerpts and comments into your Book Marketing Cheat Sheet in this format when they become available:

Book Review:
"Excerpted comments from book review."
-   Name of reviewer, Title, Publication/Website

Reader Comment:
"Comment about book."
-   Name of reader, City, State

You can take this a step further by creating memes of the best comments from your readers. Here are a couple of examples of memes we created from customer comments submitted to BookLocker.com. Notice that we also used the opportunity to promote the authors' books as well! They scratched out back, so we scratched theirs, and we were very happy to do so!

On my laptop, I keep a folder of memes specifically for posting to social media. I recommend you do the same. Creating a posting schedule for testimonial memes, and add that to your Book Marketing Cheat Sheet.

Bookmarks (no, not the printed kind)

You're going to be participating in quite a few online discussions while promoting your book and you need to remember where these discussions are taking place. Whatever you do, don't drop into a discussion, post something, and then disappear forever. This can hurt your credibility and may make it appear you just dropped by to spam the group/blog/publication.

Although some websites will notify you by email when somebody responds to one of your posts, not all do, and spam filters might eat some of the automated messages coming your way.

Furthermore, the "bookmarks" in your web browser might not be saved if you have a computer crash.

___ Day 20

Add a "Bookmarks" section to your Book Marketing Cheat Sheet, and start copying and pasting the URLs of ongoing discussions you are participating in during your online marketing activities.

Days 21–23:

Signatures

by Angela Hoy

A signature is effective, yet subtle, marketing text you can add under your name to every email you send, and also under your name when you're posting to discussion lists, blogs, or news articles online.

Unfortunately, this tool is underused or misused by many. You should absolutely use signatures to promote not only your book(s), but also your website, ezine, or blog in general. And, don't forget to promote your free ebook to continue attracting new subscribers!

EMAIL SIGNATURES

In your own email program, search the Help function for the word "signature." If you're not already familiar with this nifty gizmo, read about it in your email program. The email signature is usually easy to set up and use. Once you set it up, your email program will automatically add it to every email you send.

In your email signature you can pretty much get away with blatant self-promotion without appearing to be pushy. Here's an example. Several times each month, I send out a questionnaire to magazine editors that pay writers, asking them whether they'd like a free market listing on WritersWeekly.com. Market listings show writers what types of articles a magazine editor is interested in, how much they pay, what rights they take, etc. Lucky for me, my website targets writers, and most editors are also writers. Many editors even secretly freelance for other publications on the side to earn extra money, and have a deep desire to freelance full-time so they can work at home. So, while I'm offering their publication (their day-job) free exposure in WritersWeekly.com, the writer in them also sees my email signature, which promotes my free ebook, my website, and usually one or two of my other writing-related books.

Here's the key. It's much easier to get someone to sign up for something that's free than it is to convince them to buy your book when they first meet you. Hook them now and they'll probably buy from you later, after they get to know you through your ezine. Marketing professionals know that prospective buyers usually have to see a new product (book) several times before they'll actual buy that item. So, your primary signature should promote your FREE ezine and FREE ebook. That way, they're more likely to subscribe to your ezine and you can start exposing them to your book (via ads in your ezine) on a repeat basis, whenever you send them a new issue.

Sample Email Signature Promoting a Free Ebook

OBTAIN A FREE COPY OF *QUERY LETTERS THAT WORKED* This free ebook is available for instant download to new WritersWeekly subscribers. Sign up and receive your free book instantly right here: https://writersweekly.com/subscribe

Sample Email Signature Promoting a New Book

FREE EXCERPT
BOOK PROPOSALS THAT WORKED! Real Book Proposals That Landed $10K – $100K Publishing Contracts. Want to read real book proposals that landed these contracts? Simon and Schuster, $100,000; Berkeley Books, $25,000; Osborne-McGraw-Hill, $19,500; Random House, $15,000; and many more! See a complete list here: https://www.writersweekly.com/books/3332.html

Sample Email Signature Promoting Our Publishing Company

Since we also own BookLocker.com, I have a different email signature that promotes that service to authors. And, many writers have considered writing a book, or have already written one. Is this signature obnoxiously long? Yes, but it's an email signature so it's perfectly acceptable, and not considered spam since I only send this to folks who have previously contacted me.

PUBLISH YOUR BOOK IN 1 MONTH - $675
(add $200 if you need original cover design)

D.I.Y. PROGRAM ONLY $78

UNHAPPY WITH YOUR CURRENT P.O.D. PUBLISHER?
If you own your production files, move to BookLocker - only $268.

ALREADY A BOOKLOCKER AUTHOR? PAY ONLY $268!
(original cover design is extra)

See:
https://publishing.booklocker.com/

~ ~ ~

BookLocker is rated "OUTSTANDING" by attorney Mark Levine, author of
The Fine Print of Self Publishing

"As close to perfection as you're going to find in the world of ebook and POD
publishing. The ebook royalties are the highest I've ever seen,
and the print royalties are better than average. BookLocker understands
what new authors experience, and has put together a package that is the
best in the business. You can't go wrong here. Plus, they're selective and
won't publish any manuscript just because it's accompanied by a check.
Also, the web site is well trafficked. If you can find a POD or epublisher with
as much integrity and dedication to selling authors' books, but with lower
POD publishing fees, please let me know."

– Attorney Mark Levine, author of The Fine Print of Self-Publishing

Unsolicited BookLocker Author Testimonials:
https://publishing.booklocker.com/testimonials

Sample Combo Email Signature

Don't think you have to stop at one email signature. I often combine mine like this:

==

OBTAIN A FREE COPY OF *QUERY LETTERS THAT WORKED*
This free ebook is available for instant download to new WritersWeekly subscribers. Sign up and receive your free book instantly right here: https://writersweekly.com/subscribe

==

FREE EXCERPT
BOOK PROPOSALS THAT WORKED! Real Book Proposals That Landed $10K – $100K Publishing Contracts. Want to read real book proposals that landed these contracts? Simon and Schuster, $100,000; Berkeley Books, $25,000; Osborne-McGraw-Hill, $19,500; Random House, $15,000; and many more! See a complete list here: https://www.writersweekly.com/books/3332.html

I know. Pretty long and blatantly promotional huh? But, it works and nobody has ever complained about my email signatures in the 20+ years I've been using them.

___ Day 21

Create four different email signatures, one each to promote:

Your free ebook (per the previous chapter)
Your free ezine
Your book(s)
Your website

___ Day 22

Create a combo signature that features all or some of your signatures.

Add all of your signatures, including the combo one, to your Book Marketing Cheat Sheet.

USING SIGNATURES ON OTHER PEOPLE'S WEBSITES

The great thing about signatures is they are so popular and accepted that people use them when posting online to discussion lists/groups, blogs, news articles that allow comments, and more. However, you need to be much more subtle when using signatures on websites owned by other people or you may risk being labeled a spammer. The way to be more subtle is to have a one-line signature for each of your products/services, and to use only one when posting online - the one most appropriate to each particular post you make. Here's an example.

One of my books is called *DON'T CUT ME AGAIN! True Stories About Vaginal Birth After Cesarean (VBAC)*. When I was pregnant with our fifth child, Mason, my doctor at the time told me I "had to have a c-section" simply because I'd had one previously. My shock and subsequent research revealed what appears to be a mass conspiracy in the medical community designed to force women to have often-unnecessary surgery for the doctor's and hospital's convenience, and for their pocketbooks (c-sections are far more expensive than vaginal births).

This is a really hot topic and there is no shortage of new articles, blogs, discussion lists, and more where I can share my story in an attempt to help other women who also feel their doctor is forcing them to go under the knife.

When posting my story, my signature not only promotes my book, but also gives my words an air of authority. I'm not just a woman who had a successful VBAC. I'm also a published author.

This is the simple yet extremely effective signature I use when I'm posting VBAC comments online:

Angela Hoy
Author, *DON'T CUT ME AGAIN! True Stories About Vaginal Birth After Cesarean (VBAC)*

That's all that's needed. If anybody wants to find my book, they'll simply look it up on Amazon. And, believe me, they do, and they have no problem finding, and buying my book based on the title alone. Whenever I go on a posting binge (that's what I call it when I get caught up in the current news stories and controversy surrounding the topic), I always notice an increase in my VBAC book sales.

Come up with different, short electronic signatures that you're going to be using when you start conversing with your book's potential readers online.

___ Day 23

Create separate, one-line signatures to promote:
Your book(s)
Your free ebook
Your website
Your ezine/blog

Add these to your Book Marketing Cheat Sheet.

Days 24–25:

Your Free Book Excerpt(s)

by Angela Hoy

It goes without saying that giving away a free excerpt of your book online is far better than not offering one at all. Since readers aren't standing in a bookstore, holding your book, and able to flip through it, you need to give them the chance to do just that, but in an instantaneous, free electronic way. Although some well-known authors may disagree with me, I do not believe you should give away your entire book free in the hopes that some of those people might buy the print version later. This might work for celebrities but it's probably not going to work for you and me, especially since most people are perfectly happy to read ebooks on their computers or handheld devices now. If they are happy to have an ebook, they have no incentive whatsoever to buy the print version. In many cases, your ebook earnings can actually exceed your print book earnings (higher royalties and no printing/shipping fees), so why give away an entire ebook that people are perfectly willing to pay for after reading a free excerpt?

FICTION

Most fiction authors offer a couple or a few chapters of their novel(s) for free online. Some companies offer a huge chunk, and then leave off the last chapter or two as a tempting tease to potential fans. We have offered a few sample chapters of books as excerpts and we have offered significant portions of books as free excerpts, and we haven't noticed a difference in sales one way or the other. What we do know is that most unknown authors who give away entire versions of their book online sell fewer print books, or none at all.

We believe three chapters are sufficient. Let's be honest. If you can't hook a reader in three chapters, you need a major rewrite! Whatever you do, make sure your excerpt has an irresistible cliffhanger or information teaser at the end. You should also include a Title Page, a Copyright Page, and an About the Author page that will give the reader more personal insight into *you*. Readers love to learn more about their favorite authors and, the closer they feel to you, the better chance they're going to want to buy your book, as well as your future books.

NONFICTION

If you're a non-fiction author, you probably know that some readers are interested only in a few very specific tidbits of information from your book. In fact, some people, if they can get their hands on those specific pages in your book for free, will not buy the actual book. I absolutely do *not* recommend giving away the golden nuggets in your non-fiction book. Just offer a bit of gold dust as a teaser.

Unfortunately, if you're selling your ebook through Amazon or some other online stores, they will choose what parts of your book to display of your book as an excerpt.

For non-fiction books being promoted via your free excerpt, I would offer your introduction and perhaps a choice chapter or two, but not the golden nuggets that you know people really want, and are willing to pay for.

In your excerpt, you absolutely must include an About the Author page that shows the reader specifically what qualified you to write the book. You wouldn't believe how many finance and stock market book manuscripts we've seen with no About the Author page included! Why would anybody buy a book on finance or investments from somebody with no qualifications? So, in the excerpt, show the reader why you are the perfect person to teach them about the topic(s) your book covers.

Fiction authors should include personal information, and links to their website where readers can read more about the author's other books.

YOUR FREE EXCERPT

___ Day 24

Create a word processing document and consolidate (and attractively format) the text of your free excerpt into one file. Include these components:

A title page that includes the cover, ordering information for your book (remember to point readers to your *own* website!), and a brief marketing message.

A copyright page

An About the Author page

The actual excerpt from the book, ending with an irresistible cliffhanger or information teaser

A final page that once again includes your book's ordering information

___ Day 25

Format the document you created yesterday in three different ways:

PDF

Most computers come with software that can open and read PDF files and those are very user friendly. Here's how to do it. After formatting your excerpt in MSWord (or your favorite word processing program), convert it to PDF. Your version of MSWord might already have a pdf converter in it. You can also use this free service:
https://acrobat.adobe.com/us/en/free-trial-download.html

You can see an example of my free PDF excerpt here:
https://assets.booklocker.com/pdfs/1409s.pdf

You can see many other examples of formatted PDF excerpts at:
https://www.BookLocker.com.

TEXT ONLY

Save the excerpt you created yesterday in your word processing program as a text-only file. Clean up the formatting and save that to your Book Marketing Cheat Sheet.

TEXT ONLY & EMAIL FRIENDLY

Some ezines are still sent out in text-only mode (not HTML). Save another copy of your text-only excerpt. You're going to use it to create an email friendly excerpt (short lines of text with blank lines between paragraphs). Try to make it look like an article. You should include a title and a notice that it is an excerpt, like this:

HOW TO FIND EMPLOYERS WHO HIRE WRITERS,
BUT WHO DON'T RUN EMPLOYMENT ADS
by Angela Hoy

Excerpted from *QUERY LETTERS THAT WORKED!*
Real Queries That Landed $2K+ Writing Assignments

This type of short-line text formatting, which I'm using
right here, is good for sharing your excerpt with ezines
that are distributed by email. If you supply a free excerpt
to an ezine owner, pre-formatted to be email-friendly, and
resembling an article (with a title, subtitle, and author
bio), she/he will love you for it and your chances of
publication in their periodical will be much higher.

Save the text-only, email-friendly version of your excerpt to your Book Marketing Cheat Sheet.

Days 26–30:

Posting Your Book Excerpt Online

WHERE SHOULD YOU POST OR SEND YOUR EXCERPT?

Your own website

Your publisher's website

Your colleagues' websites. Email your friends, family, and colleagues, and ask whether they'll post a link to the excerpt on your website, or your entire excerpt on their website or in their ezine. Don't forget to offer to do something for them in return!

___ Day 26

Add a page to your website offering the free excerpt of your book. Be sure to add a link to the excerpt on all your website pages.

Ask your publisher to post your free excerpt on their website if they're not already featuring one.

Run a teaser to your online excerpt in the next issue (and every subsequent issue!) of your ezine, and link to the online excerpt when you do.

___ Day 27

Ask friends, relatives, colleagues, and fellow writers who have websites if they'll post your excerpt on their websites and/or run teasers about your excerpt in their own publications (which will send readers to the link featured in your excerpt!). Be prepared to offer to do the same for them.

Free Article Websites and Distribution Services

We know what you're thinking. Why should I give away free content when I usually write for money? What we're talking about here is not original content. Far from it. Free article sites offer directories of promotional content disguised as feature articles. Most of these sites readily acknowledge that the content they offer is promotional so you should never offer original content for which you would normally get paid to write.

There are hundreds of these free article sites online now. Basically, this is how it works. Somebody writes a promotional article (like your excerpt), and posts it online. Publishers can pull the articles from those websites, and publish them free, provided they include the entire article and your byline. We have used these types of sites, and publication of my excerpts on some of them did indeed result in book sales. Below are some of the most popular free article sites. At the end are two sites that serve as distribution services to free article websites, and also to publishers, ezines, and more. Although we were initially fearful of spam threats, we did use one of these services and they did distribute one of our promotional articles (an excerpt) far and wide. It was a whole lot easier than manually posting to each free article website, and we didn't get any spam complaints at all. Of course, we can't guarantee that you won't.

ATTENTION FICTION AUTHORS

If you want to publish something promotional at the websites in this chapter, you will need to offer them non-fiction content. Perhaps you have some advice for other fiction writers on your website that you can spin into an "article" for free distribution, or maybe you have previously written about the history behind your book idea? Maybe you can profile yourself, meaning turning your bio into a third-person essay? Again, although we don't advocate offering original content to these sites, if you already have non-fiction content that you can use to point people to your website, that's perfect.

FREE ARTICLE WEBSITES

In addition to the ones listed below, you can find even more of these sites by searching your favorite search engine for "free articles."

___ Day 28

Post your free excerpt or article to these sites:

Family Features
https://editors.familyfeatures.com/

Ezine Articles
https://ezinearticles.com/submit/

ArticleGeek.com
http://www.articlegeek.com/editorial_guidelines.htm

Articles Factory
http://www.articlesfactory.com/submit.html

Amazines
https://www.amazines.com/register.cfm

Copyright Free Content
https://www.copyrightfreecontent.com/copyright-free-articles/

___ Day 29

Post your free excerpt or article to these sites:

ArticlesBase
https://articlesbase.com/submit-article/

ArticleBiz.com
https://articlebiz.com/submitArticle

ArticleCity
https://www.articlecity.com/article_submission.php

ARTICLE DISTRIBUTION SERVICES

___ Day 30

If you have some spare change, and want someone to do the posting for you, check out:
https://www.bigfoot.marketing/article_distribution_services_for_small_businesses.php

There is also software you can download that distributes articles (your excerpt) far and wide. Check out this list:
https://seotipsandsolution.com/best-article-submission-software/

Day 31:

Getting Your Book Reviewed!

It's never too late to ask somebody to review your book. Although it may be tempting to try to get your book reviewed by a celebrity, you might have to wait months or even years for that "review" to arrive, if it arrives at all.

You can even ask professional colleagues to read and write reviews of your book(s), but you might be forced to wait too long for those reviews too.

From my experience, with the exception of big-name celebrities, the review itself, not the name under it, is what helps sell a book. An honest book review by someone in your writing group, or even a friend or neighbor who honestly enjoyed your book, is better than no review at all. Just be sure it's an honest review.

You should never, *ever* pay any individual or company to review your book. There's no faster way to ruin your reputation as an author than posting a glowing review about your book that you paid someone to write.

___ Day 31

Find five or ten people who might be willing to review your book. When one agrees, send them a free print copy if applicable. Don't be cheap and offer an ebook only. Most people still do prefer reading entire books in print.

Ask them to please read and review the book within the next month or so, and email the review to you. You can also ask them to post the review to Amazon.com, and the other major online bookstores. Be sure to ask their permission to republish the review in your marketing materials.

When reviews start coming in, add excerpts from the best ones to your Book Marketing Cheat Sheet, and post them to your website, your ezine, your publisher's website, BarnesandNoble.com, Amazon.com, and other large bookstore websites where your book is for sale. If your publisher uses Ingram, the distributor (BookLocker DOES), you can ask them to post the reviews in Ingram's system. Those will then be distributed to Ingram's retail partners, including Amazon, BN.com, and many others.

If you get a really stunning quote from a reader, publish a few of their words in your email signature!

Again, remember to add the text of the best ones to your Book Marketing Cheat Sheet so you'll have them readily available during your marketing activities, and keep adding them in the future as different fans write to you over the months and years.

If you publish a revised edition of your book in the future, you can add quotes from reviewers to the back cover, or to the first page on the inside to tempt potential buyers. NOTE: When people see your book online, they can't see the back cover. That's why we recommend adding review excerpts to the very first page if your book.

For more information, see:
How to EASILY Get Awesome and Honest Book Reviews That REALLY Carry Weight With Readers!

Day 32:

Reader Comments = Marketing Blurbs

Positive reader comments that appear on bookstore pages online are very powerful motivators for potential readers of a particular book. Instead of actual book reviews, these are personal notes about the book that are usually sent to the author.

Ask readers, via your website and your newsletter, and even during the ordering process on your website (if you're processing your own orders), to submit their comments about your book to you by email, or through an automated form on your website.

At BookLocker.com, we send out an automated email to every customer after they purchase a book. We send out this email 1 day after they buy an ebook, and 10 days after they buy a print book. The short email thanks them for their purchase, and asks them for feedback on the transaction. We've received lots of valuable comments from readers over the years. Doing so lets the customer know we care, and we and the author receives feedback about their book.

___ Day 32

On your website, in your ezine, and even in your book itself (in the email edition and, if it's not yet published, the print edition as well), ask readers to contact you with comments after reading your book. They can either email their comments to you or they can submit comments through a form you can create on your website. When they do, ask for permission to quote them in your future marketing materials.

You'll be surprised how many happy readers really want to help authors (and connect with them directly!) by submitting positive or otherwise helpful comments about a book. If they give you permission to quote them in your marketing materials, you'll start to have quite a collection of reader recommendations for your book!

Excerpt/quote from the best ones in your Book Marketing Cheat Sheet so you'll have them readily available during your marketing activities.

Days 33–34:

Enhancing Your Amazon.com Book Page

Now that you have your handy Book Marketing Cheat Sheet pretty full, you can start using it to promote your book, website, ezine and free ebook on a variety of websites. Let's start with the largest online retailer.

If your book was traditionally published, or published by one of the large POD publishers, it is for sale on Amazon. Beware of POD publishers who don't partner with Ingram, the largest book distributor who sends an automated electronic feed to numerous online bookstores, including Amazon. Most bookstores prefer to order from Ingram directly, so it is imperative that your book be included in their electronic catalog. Ingram ships many books directly to Amazon's customers, even using an Amazon.com return address label!

If your book isn't on Amazon.com, your publisher sucks. Sorry, but it's true. If your publisher can't or won't list your book on Amazon, find another publisher!

You can list your book on Amazon yourself but you will not only need to give them a bigger percentage of the sale (a very unreasonable 55%-65%, which is much more than if it were in Ingram's system), but you'll also have to ship books to Amazon, pay for shipping (and return shipping if they don't sell), and pay them an annual fee as well. We heard Amazon may also now be charging these types of accounts a fee for each book they have on their shelves for more than a year. This is the Amazon Advantage Program. We call it the Amazon Dis-Advantage Program.

At BookLocker.com, all our print books are in Ingram's feed, and are automatically listed on Amazon.com, BarnesandNoble.com, BooksAMillion.com, Chapters.indigo.ca, Walmart.com, and numerous other online bookstores worldwide, many of which you've probably never even heard of. (Disclaimer: Any bookstore can, at their discretion, refuse to list or cease listing any book at any time.) Any store that has an Ingram account can pick up Ingram's automated feed. They have thousands of retail customers across the globe.

Through their automated feed, Ingram only distributes the bare minimum in book listing information (cover, list price, page count, short description, etc.) to those stores so your excerpt and other descriptive information may not be posted there. Adding it should be easy. Unfortunately, some of the stores make it a bit difficult to find what you need to add anything at all. So, we've done the research for you. Here you go.

___ Day 33

Amazon.com

Go to https://authorcentral.amazon.com/gp/home

Set up your Author Central account, where you can then add images, lists of your book, you bio, and much more.

___ Day 34

On Amazon's page for your book, upload images, and even a video, like a book trailer! If anyone has asked questions about your book on Amazon, you can answer them on that page as well.

If you need to update your book description, or anything else appearing on your actual book page on Amazon, ask your publisher to do that through Ingram's automated system. Doing this will ensure the update is made across the board, on all of the websites for Ingram's retail customers.

Days 35–36:

Enhancing Your Book's Presence on Other Major Online Bookstores

As you did in the previous chapter, you're going to enhance your book pages on the other major online bookstore websites using the information in your Book Marketing Cheat Sheet. If your book is in Ingram's feed, it probably appears on these sites as well.

___ Day 35

BarnesandNoble.com
1. Go to https://www.barnesandnoble.com/
2. At the very bottom of the page, click Publisher & Author Guidelines.
3. Click How to Submit Content
4. Be sure to then click on the link titled "Preparing Text"

___ Day 36

BooksaMillion.com
1. Go to https://www.booksamillion.com/
2. At the bottom of the page, click For Authors & Publishers
3. Click Additional content
4. Read the section titled Submitting additional content

Other online retailers have similar options for enhancing your book page on their sites.

You should check your books' pages in the major online bookstores at least every month or so to ensure everything is working correctly and also to see whether readers are posting reviews.

Days 37–41:

Cozying Up to Sites with a Good Google Ranking

by Angela Hoy

Over the next few days, we're going to expand our online marketing reach by cozying up to websites, ezines, and blogs that have good Google rankings! Not all of us are lucky enough to have our website, ezine, blog, or book page show up near the top of the search results when somebody Googles specific keywords. Why not rub shoulders with those who do?

We are always interested in publishing book excerpts for (and articles by) readers of WritersWeekly.com (who are writers). If anyone sends us a quality book excerpt from a writing-related book that matches our editorial vision (https://writersweekly.com/writersweekly-com-writers-guidelines), we'll not only publish it, along with their bio and links to their website, blog, ezine, or book, but we'll pay them for it as well. Likewise, if somebody submits a query letter who is the author of a writing-related book, and if their article idea matches our needs, we'll buy and publish their article, and publish links to their website, blog, ezine, or book on our website. Since we are affiliates on Amazon.com and BarnesandNoble.com, we can post links to those websites where we can earn a bit of affiliate income if one of our readers clicks to buy someone else's book that they found on our website.

Now, I'm not saying that all websites and ezines will pay you for your contribution. Some do, but many don't, especially if they know you're promoting your book in the process. And, although we don't advocate writing for free, we do advocate distributing reprinted editorial content, like book excerpts, that can get you free advertising.

So, remember that excerpt you wrote and formatted previously? Let's see where else we can get that published, and let's also see whether we can get some people to link to your book on Amazon!

NON-FICTION AUTHORS

There really is no other way to explain this to you other than showing you by example. We'll use my book, *QUERY LETTERS THAT WORKED! Real Queries That Landed $2K+ Writing Assignments* (https://writersweekly.com/books/1409.html) as an example for this exercise. Read below to see how this works, and then use your own keywords from your Book Marketing Cheat Sheet to do this exercise for your own book(s).

If you were a writer looking for tips on how to write a query letter, what keywords would you use in Google? Perhaps these:

query letter
queries
freelance writing
freelance writers
writing for magazines

(Refer back to the chapter titled *Finding the Keywords Your Potential Readers Are Really Using Online,* and also see your Book Marketing Cheat Sheet for your own keywords.)

For this exercise, we're just going to use the first keyword as an example. Over the next few days, you're going to do the following exercise with your top five keywords appearing in your Book Marketing Cheat Sheet. Sure, you can use more than five if you want! The more websites you contact, the more exposure you'll get.

Okay, go to Google.com, and type in your top keyword or phrase. When we Googled *query letter*, these were the top 10 sites that popped up:

1. http://johnhewitt.blog/how-to-write-a-query-letter/
Ooh! I am IN LUCK! This is a site that allows readers to post comments under the featured articles. I could easily and instantly post a professional comment about the article here, and subtly promote myself by signing my name like this:

Angela Hoy, Author
QUERY LETTERS THAT WORKED! Real Queries That Landed $2K+ Writing Assignments

Anybody reading my comment and signature could easily find my book for sale online at a variety of bookstores.

2. https://www.janefriedman.com/query-letters/
Like with #1 above, this site also allows comments under each article. Bingo!!

3. https://blog.reedsy.com/how-to-write-a-query-letter/
Ditto! I'm having GREAT luck with these today!!

4. https://nybookeditors.com/2015/12/how-to-write-a-darn-good-query-letter/

While this article is a few years old, there are 90 comments underneath it. So, not only can I comment as well but, since the article is #4 on Google, that means people are coming to it, and will keep coming to it.

HINT: Never be afraid to post a differing point of view under an article or blog post. Doing so can generate a lot of discussion and, subsequently, more publicity. Just be aware that the owner of the site can filter posts, and can also make debates sway one way or the other by allowing only specific comments from readers, or even by editing readers' comments. Yes, I've caught unscrupulous bloggers doing this on a few occasions.

If any of the sites I'm posting comments to are also selling books with Amazon links, I can approach them, and ask them to list my book, too, knowing they'll receive affiliate income for any sales resulting from that link.

My email would look something like this:

Hi there,

I'm mentioning your site in WritersWeekly.com this week in an article for my series on online book marketing.

I was wondering whether you'd be interested in adding one of my books to your website as one of your Amazon affiliate links?

My book is:
QUERY LETTERS THAT WORKED! Real Queries That Landed $2K+ Writing Assignments

The Amazon page is:
https://www.amazon.com/LETTERS-WORKED-queries-writing-assignments/dp/159113384X

You could add your Amazon affiliate link to the end of that.

Have a beautiful day!

Angela Hoy
WritersWeekly.com

5. https://www.writing-world.com/menus/queries.shtml

This is a highly-respected website run by Moira Allen. I could send Moira an email offering her these options:

a. She could run an excerpt of my book for free in her ezine or on her website
b. She could add the electronic version of my ebook to her online bookstore because she sells ebooks and she could then pay me royalties
c. She could add links on her site to Amazon.com, and earn affiliate income if she wants

I might also offer Moira an original article on query letters because she is a paying market for writers. I would, of course, promote my book in my bio, which would appear at the end of the article.

6. https://writersdigestshop.com/pages/the-query-letter

Ah! I just struck gold! This is the most popular writing magazine. And, they pay writers! I can pitch articles to them and, of course, promote my own websites and books in my byline.

7. http://www.eclectics.com/articles/query.html
This is another respected website for writers. I could email them and ask whether they'd be interested in adding an affiliate link to my book's Amazon page at their URL. I'm also tickled to discover they have a very active message board! I can instantly join, and start participating in discussions with their readers who are writers and, thus, my target audience. As long as I am a valued participant, offering professional advice without a promotional push, and only including my name book title in my signature, nobody is likely to accuse me of spamming the board.

8. https://en.wikipedia.org/wiki/Query_letter
Wikipedia is a *very* popular website! I went there, and found three links to other sites at the bottom. The top one is a blog that allows comments to be posted. Jackpot! The second and third links are ones I had previously found on Google.

9 and 10. Hmmm. These are two books on Amazon about Query Letters and they're popping up above my book's Amazon listing on Google. Why? This is an obvious indicator that I need to revise my search words on Amazon. Yes, revising your book's description on Amazon to be more attractive to Google is online book marketing! I'm going to go to the two book pages that are popping up, and see what their keywords are on Amazon. If I pull up the Amazon page for these books in my browser, I can then right-click the button on my mouse, and click View Page Source.

The page that pops up is html, and is very difficult to navigate. So, I will click to search the page for this: meta name="keywords" content="

I can see what keywords and phrases those authors/publishers are using on Amazon to promote their books. I will need to revise my keywords so my book's Amazon.com page will pop up higher in Google! How will I do that? I will change the keywords in my Ingram listing. If you need to do this, send your new keywords to your publisher so they can update those in Ingram's system. Those will then feed into Amazon's database, as well as other retailers' sites.

FICTION

Not to worry, fiction authors. There are plenty of fun Googling activities for you to do like this, too!

Unfortunately, I haven't written any novels—I'm saving that for retirement—but I can use another novelist as an example. Scott Rose is a respected journalist and the author of the mystery *Death in Hawaii* as well as *Mr. David Cooper's Happy Suicide*. For *Death in Hawaii*, the basic words that somebody (perhaps a vacationer looking for a beach book?) might Google for a novel like this, which is set in Hawaii, could be *fiction Hawaii*.

Remember, you need to use the top five keywords appearing on your Book Marketing Cheat Sheet. But for this example, I'm only going to use one.

When I search for *fiction Hawaii* on Google, here's what pops up at the top:

1. https://blog.sfgate.com/hawaii/2009/07/30/modern-moolelo-your-favorite-hawaii-fiction/
We've hit gold! This is a popular news site (*San Francisco Chronicle*) and they have an entire page of Hawaii fiction on their site. What's more, they allow comments to be posted underneath the article! If I were Scott, I would post a helpful comment here while subtly promoting my book in my signature.

2. http://www.honolulumagazine.com/Honolulu-Magazine/May-2018/50-Hawaii-Books-You-Should-Read-in-Your-Lifetime/
Yea!! Not only was Honolulu Magazine interested enough in books about Hawaii to make a list of the top 50, but they allow comments under the article. A smart author would definitely take the opportunity to subtly promote their own books there!

3. The third result is a library page. While it's tempting to email the library to see whether they'll buy a copy, doing so would be spam. Skip that.

4. https://www.johann-sandra.com/hawaii/books/
The Hawaii Bookstore! When you click on a book, it takes you to the website owner's Amazon affiliate links. If I were Scott, I would contact the owner and ask them to add my book to their website. Again, see 4 under non-fiction above.

5. http://archives.starbulletin.com/2007/08/07/features/story02.html
Hmm! A book review for a Hawaii-related novel by Michael Egan in the *Honolulu Star-Bulletin*! Scott should definitely send the book reviewer a very short email about *Death in Hawaii*, and ask whether he'd like to receive a print copy for review. Sending review copies without asking permission can result in a waste of money. Asking permission first means you won't be paying to send copies to a reviewer who might just toss the book, but also increases your chances of actually getting a review from the reviewer who does express initial interest. The personal touch is always the best.

Please see "Throwing Away Your Money on Review Copies?" at: https://writersweekly.com/angela-desk/throwing-away-your-money-on-review-copies-

Are you ready to get started? Okay, open your Book Marketing Cheat Sheet, and pull up your top five keywords or phrases.

___ Day 37

Perform the exercise above using the first set of five keywords or phrases appearing on your Book Marketing Cheat Sheet. Individually contact the top 10 websites that appear in your search results. And, just like I did above, skip the ones that are not a good match for you.

___ Day 38

You should have 25 keywords or phrases in your Book Marketing Cheat Sheet. Perform the exercise above using the second group of five keywords or phrases. Individually contact the top 10 websites that appear in your search results. Skip the ones that are not a good match for you.

___ Day 39

Perform the exercise above using the third group of five keywords or phrases appearing on your Book Marketing Cheat Sheet. Individually contact the top 10 websites that appear in your search results. Skip the ones that are not a good match for you.

___ Day 40

Perform the exercise above using the fourth group of five keywords or phrases appearing on your Book Marketing Cheat Sheet. Individually contact the top 10 websites that appear in your search results. Skip the ones that are not a good match for you.

___ Day 41

Perform the exercise above using the fifth group of five keywords or phrases appearing on your Book Marketing Cheat Sheet. Individually contact the top 10 websites that appear in your search results. Skip the ones that are not a good match for you.

+ This is an ongoing activity. Please refer to "AFTER 90 DAYS: YOUR BOOK'S DAILY MARKETING PLAN" near the end of this book.

Days 42–46:

Free Advertising for You /
Free Content for Them

Now it's time to drum up some free advertising in ezines, blogs, websites, and maybe even some magazines.

If you can't or won't spend money to place ads in magazines, ezines, blogs, and websites, you might still be able to get them to mention your book. How? By offering free content for them to publish.

Remember the book excerpts we formatted earlier (see your Book Marketing Cheat Sheet)? Well, let's see whether we can get those published in some periodicals that are already serving your book's target audience.

We will use Angela's *BOOK PROPOSALS THAT WORKED! Real Book Proposals That Landed $10K - $100K Publishing Contracts* as an example in this chapter. Follow along with us, but use your book instead.

THE INITIAL PITCH

We're going to come up with a simple form letter that we will personalize, and send to the editor or publisher of each periodical. We will then add that form letter to our Book Marketing Cheat Sheet so we'll have easy access to it during this and future marketing activities. We've found that a very personal, friendly approach works best for us but you might want to make yours a bit more formal, depending on the topic of your book. Our letter will look something like this:

Hi [name of editor/publisher/blogger],

This is Angela Hoy, publisher of WritersWeekly.com and author of *BOOK PROPOSALS THAT WORKED! Real Book Proposals That Landed $10K - $100K Publishing Contracts.*

I was wondering whether you'd like to run a free excerpt of my book in your [newsletter/magazine/blog/website/etc.]. I would be very happy to send you the excerpt as well as a free electronic copy of the entire book for your review.

My book appears on Amazon.com so, if you are an Amazon affiliate, you can use your Amazon affiliate link in or under the excerpt if you prefer.

If you have any questions, I'm right here.

Have a beautiful day!

Angela

FOLLOW UP WHEN THEY BITE

When they bite, you want to be ready with a short, personalized form letter so you can gently urge them to take action while they're still interested. Our follow-up would look something like this:

Hi [editor's first name],

Thanks so much for responding so quickly! Please find attached the free excerpt. It's in text-only format for your convenience. If you need it in a different format, no problem. Just let me know. You can publish the excerpt freely in your publication and/or on your website.

If you have an Amazon affiliate account, you can point your readers to that link instead of to my website. That way, you'll make some money each time one of your readers buys a copy.

If you want a free copy of the actual ebook (not the excerpt, but the entire book) for your own use, it is 1.2 megs. Is it okay to email a PDF file of that size to you or do you want me to put it on our server for you to download?

Have a super afternoon!

Angela

FINDING THE PERIODICALS

1. Let's go to Google.com (yes, again), and try to find ezines, websites, blogs, magazines, newsletters, or any periodical that might be serving your target readers. For this exercise, we're going to type in some keywords and phrases along with one type of publication at a time. We will then use the top five results. When doing this exercise for your book, you will want to use a variety of keywords and phrases, and contact at least ten different companies. The more, the better!

For Angela's book, we're looking for periodicals that serve writers so we're going to type the top five keywords or phrases into Google for her book:

"freelance writers" blog
"freelance writers" ezine
"freelance writers" newsletter
"freelance writers" magazine
"freelance writers" website

We can also spin this into other keywords (like "freelance writing," "new authors," and more), thus ensuring we have an almost unlimited supply of periodicals to approach.

Okay, Google, here we come.

Results for "freelance writers" blog:
1. https://www.theblogstarter.com/

This is a page advertising a book on how to start a blog. Not only can we contact this site to offer free contents, but it allows comments underneath each article.

2. https://thefreelancersyear.com/blog/best-freelance-writing-blogs/
http://freelancewrite.about.com/
Similar to the example above, we can offer them free content and also post comments under a few posts on the blog. We could spend weeks posting comments here but we won't do that because the owner of the site would get upset. Instead, we'll post a comment under the article at the link above, and will look for one or two other popular articles on that site.

3. https://allfreelancewriting.com/blog/
This is another popular freelance writing blog that might be interested in free content from us, but that allows comments under posts. We can subtly promote Angela's books and our websites in our signatures after contributing to the conversations occurring there.

4. https://www.freelancerfaqs.com/freelance-writing-blogs/
Not only is this a popular site in itself that allows comments under posts, but this specific page lists other popular blogs for writers. So, we could spend an entire day offering free content to those websites while also promoting Angela's books and our websites using comment marketing under the posts on those blogs.

5. https://www.makealivingwriting.com/stop-writing-blog-posts-do-this-instead/
This is a popular site that might be interested in articles from us. The comments are closed on this particular article. Bummer. However, since blogs appear online with posts sorted newest to oldest, and knowing this is a popular site with lots of comments by readers in the past, we can click on the "blog" link at the top of the page, look at the most recent blog posts, and add comments under those.

After we finish marketing the heck out of Angela's books and our websites using "freelancer writer" blog, we would then Google the rest of the terms ("freelance writers" ezine, "freelance writers" newsletter, etc.) and perform the same steps as explained above.

___ Day 42 +

Complete the exercise above using the first set of keywords or phrases appearing on your Book Marketing Cheat Sheet, along with one type of periodical (i.e. "your keywords" magazine), as we did above. Individually contact the top 10 websites that appear in your search results. As in the last chapter, skip the ones that are not a good match for you.

___ Day 43 +

Complete the exercise above using the first set of keywords or phrases appearing on your Book Marketing Cheat Sheet along with *a different type of periodical* (i.e. "your keywords" blog). Individually contact the top 10 websites that appear in your search results and, again, skip the ones that are not a good match for you.

___ Day 44 +

Complete the exercise above using the second set of keywords or phrases appearing on your Book Marketing Cheat Sheet and one type of periodical (i.e. "your keywords" magazine), as we did above. Individually contact the top 10 websites that appear in your search results. As in the last chapter, skip the ones that are not a good match for you.

___ Day 45 +

Complete the exercise above using your second set of keywords or phrases appearing on your Book Marketing Cheat Sheet with *a different type of periodical* (i.e. "your keywords" blog). Individually contact the top 10 websites that appear in your search results and, again, skip the ones that are not a good match for you.

You can also try this activity with other publication terms as well (i.e. ezine, zine, magazine, etc.)

___ **Day 46 +**

You should be familiar enough with this activity to make more contacts in a shorter timeframe today. Complete the exercise above using the third set of keywords or phrases appearing on your Book Marketing Cheat Sheet and one type of periodical (i.e. "your keywords" magazine), as we did above. Individually contact the top 10 websites that appear in your search results. Skip the ones that are not a good match for you.

Next, complete the exercise above using your third set of keywords or phrases appearing on your Book Marketing Cheat Sheet with *a different type of periodical* (i.e. "your keywords" blog). Individually contact the top 10 websites that appear in your search results and, again, skip the ones that are not a good match for you.

You can also try this activity with other publication terms as well (i.e. ezine, zine, magazine, etc.)

+ This is an ongoing activity. Please refer to "AFTER 90 DAYS: YOUR BOOK'S DAILY MARKETING PLAN" near the end of this book.

Days 47–49:

Social Networking!

by Angela Hoy

Back in the day, whenever people wanted to connect with like minds online, they'd venture to the online groups and discussion boards, like groups.Google.com, groups.Yahoo.com, and lists.Topica.com.

However, those text-based conversations weren't very attractive, nor terribly easy to navigate, and there were so many of them that you could easily run into somebody interesting, and then never hear from them again. You also really didn't know who you were talking to online, which made it a bit scary. Social networking sites today do allow anonymity, but it's much easier to reconnect with people because they each have dedicated links on those social media websites.

Social media, which has *completely* changed the way we connect with others. And, it has made online marketing soooooo much easier!

FACEBOOK
https://www.facebook.com/

I originally created a personal page on Facebook just to keep an eye on our teenagers. (I made them accept me as a "friend" so I could monitor what they were posting online, and what other people were posting back to them.)

Boy, was I surprised when I started getting notifications from Facebook saying people I knew were asking me to add them as my friends list. These were WritersWeekly readers, BookLocker authors, and, of course, friends and family.
The top dog of social networking, of course, is Facebook, which allows not only personal accounts, but also free community and

71

business (i.e. "Group") accounts. All of this has turned this site into a marketer's dream.

You can:

- Promote your book to your friends, family, and fans (if you allow your fans to view your personal Facebook page)

- Promote your book to your fans via a "group" page

- Promote your book via other people's and groups' Facebook pages, including major media Facebook pages and groups

- Upload images of your book and yourself to your Facebook page, and post links to your website, your free excerpt(s), promotional videos, and much more.

- Buy advertisements at nominal fees to attract people you'd never have reached otherwise

If you get a bit overzealous in marketing through your Facebook posts, you might just lose some of your "Friends." You need to be more careful when promoting yourself on other people's Facebook pages and groups because you can be labeled a spammer, and can even lose your Facebook account.

Although you probably already have a personal Facebook page, you need to know that they currently have a 5,000-friend limit (with an unlimited number of followers), so you should still direct all people to your own personal website and your own ezine in your marketing activities. However, you can also use Facebook to promote your website, ezine, and book(s).

If you don't yet have a Facebook account, get one here: https://www.facebook.com/

You must have an account to see the examples I'll give you here.

Many personal Facebook users keep a lot of their information private, including pictures, their contact information, and posts on their "wall." If you are using Facebook to promote yourself, I strongly recommend creating what I call a "personal business Facebook page." I have an actual personal Facebook page under my maiden name where I connect with family and personal friends. However, my mother used to post baby pictures there, and I may have posted a few political comments over the years that might turn off my customers, which is always a bad idea.

So, several years ago I created my "personal business Facebook page." It's under my current name, and it's very easy for authors, writers, and other industry professionals to find me on there. On that page, I avoid political comments and anything else controversial because, when you post that stuff, you're guaranteed to anger around 50% of your "friends." Also, my mom can't post baby pictures there, nor ones from my awkward teenage years.

You can see my "personal business Facebook page" at the link below, and I'd love it if you sent me a friend request!

https://www.facebook.com/angela.hoy.750

Below are some examples of authors who are successfully using Facebook to promote themselves.

Douglas Clegg
https://www.facebook.com/DouglasClegg/

Best-selling and prolific horror and fantasy novelist Douglas Clegg uses Facebook to post notes about books he's reading, movies he's watching, the writing life in general (he allows his Facebook "friends" to ask him questions about writing fiction and the writing business), and even to promote other authors. Every once in awhile, he'll throw in a small post about a book review he received or he'll run a contest, giving away a free iPod or some other goodie to one of his ezine subscribers. That's one of the ways he uses Facebook to get new subscribers for his ezine. Oh, and there is plenty of personal stuff there, too, like pictures of his adorable dog and his amazing garden.

It's always important to share personal posts with your "friends" because people who feel a personal connection with you are far more likely to buy your books!

I encourage you to "like" Doug's page to see a master of subtle self-promotion at work. In case you don't remember, Doug Clegg was the first author to offer a free e-serial online, via email, long before even Stephen King gave it a try. If you post a note to Doug, he will personally respond. That's just one of the reasons his fans love him!

Mark LaFlamme
https://www.facebook.com/marklaflamme1

Mark LaFlamme is a hoot. He posts the most bizarre, interactive, and even shocking statements and questions on his Facebook page. His fans can't help but want to answer his questions, and post comments back to him. He has thousands of friends on Facebook, and very rarely mentions his books but, instead, subtly promotes his own website by posting it on his Facebook profile. Add Mark to your Facebook friends list and I guarantee you will be laughing almost daily at his antics! (Warning: He does post some mature comments and some may be offended.)

If you don't yet have a Facebook page designed to promote your website, ezine and book(s), it's time to get one. If you do have one, you need to be using it daily to seek out potential readers promote your website, ezine and book(s).

___ Day 47 +

Get a Facebook account *or* start promoting yourself using your existing Facebook account. Be careful if you plan to use your personal Facebook page for business. If you have potentially, personal embarrassing posts on your Facebook page, or if you've gotten overtly political at times, it's best to start a brand new Facebook page to promote your website, newsletter, and books.

Once you set up your account (which is very easy), there are a variety of ongoing marketing activities you can do on Facebook:

Solicit new friends daily. Start by looking at your friends' friends. If a particular person's page is public, you can view some of their recent posts, and then click to add them as a friend. Be sure to include a personal note so they'll know how you found them. Be professional, and mention something relevant to their recent posts so they won't think you're a creep or a stalker.

Google your favorite authors, and then find links to their Facebook accounts to request being added to their friends lists. Using Facebook's search box isn't very helpful unless you know the author's account name. Usually it's just their name, but not always, and people with identical names are permitted on Facebook so it helps to have the direct link, which many people do feature on their websites. When in doubt, you can always email them to ask. Facebook's search box does indeed work very well on occasion. A search for Danielle Steel brought up the author's group page right on top and she has hundreds of thousands of "likes"!

You can post helpful or even flattering comments under posts on your favorite authors' or other celebrities' Facebook pages while subtly promoting your book(s), website, ezine, etc.

Search for Facebook "Groups" that might be interested in your book(s). Click to "like" a particular group and then you can post messages to their pages, which can be seen by everybody else who "likes" that group. As long as you're contributing quality and helpful comments, nobody should accuse you of spamming.

When promoting my VBAC book, I found several VBAC groups on Facebook. I clicked the "Like" box at the top of them and I was then able to post congratulations notes to new moms who'd had successful VBACs, while also participating in lively discussions about the topic. Of course, I'd sign my name under each post, and include the word author and the name of my book.

You might want to consider creating a Group on Facebook under your business name or your book's general topic as well to garner even more attention for your books.

Twitter
http://www.twitter.com

Twitter is another extremely popular social networking site. If you use Twitter, you can gather far more "followers" by posting quality "Tweets" (a word that simply refers to posts on Twitter). Don't anger your followers by only posting promotional items about yourself and your book(s). If you must promote, do it subtly while posting informative Tweets. Links to articles you post to your website or blog will lead to far more clicks than outright promotion of your website, newsletter, and books. Also, more people will be interested in posting comments under your Tweets if you do that.

If you're curious, here's my Twitter page:
https://twitter.com/AngelaHoy

Doug Clegg's Twitter page is here:
https://twitter.com/DouglasClegg

___ Day 48 +

Get a Twitter account *or* start promoting yourself using your existing Twitter account. If your existing Twitter account is too personal, start one to promote your business, and use that for your marketing activities instead.

___ Day 49 +

Add links to your Facebook and Twitter accounts to your website, ezine, and email signature, and even to your About the Author pages on your future books.

WORD OF CAUTION: Social Networking is so personal that it can literally consume your entire day. You might create a controversial post, or read a post about one item, and repost it on your page. You might then get comments (positive and/or negative) that might ignite a debate, which may then lead to you posting responses for hours on end. I have, personally, had blood pressure problems during some online debates so, if you do enter into a controversial discussion, beware. You might have a hard time getting anything else done that day! The good news is, the more controversial the debate, the more people will be reading it!

And, remember that anything you post to your business accounts can be seen by just about anyone so be careful when posting in anger! Don't let your temper come back to bite your reputation later. If it's something you wouldn't say to someone's face, don't post it online.

+ This is an ongoing activity. Please refer to "AFTER 90 DAYS: YOUR BOOK'S DAILY MARKETING PLAN" near the end of this book.

WARNING

Never, *ever* agree to meet a "fan" in person! Criminals use social networking to lure and harm victims.

Days 50–51:

Promoting Your Book and Book Trailer on YouTube.com

by Angela Hoy

Posting Comments on YouTube

Shortly after releasing my book, *DON'T CUT ME AGAIN! True Stories About Vaginal Birth After Cesarean (VBAC),* I was spending an evening watching videos of VBACs on YouTube. Yeah, women really do post videos of themselves giving birth online. Don't worry. You won't find any of *my* birth videos there! However, watching other women giving birth always gets me teary-eyed.

After viewing each video, I would post comments about the video for the new mom. ("What a beautiful baby girl!" or "Oh my gosh! What a great water birth!" or "Congrats on your successful VBAC!")

Don't get the wrong idea. This is a subject I am deeply passionate about. I would never post a comment online that I didn't mean. You shouldn't either or you'll risk looking like a phony (or be accused of spamming). However, as long as I was spending my evening watching videos, and sending other moms positive notes about their VBACs, I might as well let them know I've had a VBAC, too, by posting the fact in my signature, right? So, under each of my comments, I copied and pasted my very simple signature (taken from my Book Marketing Cheat Sheet, of course), which looks like this:

Angela Hoy
Author, DON'T CUT ME AGAIN! True Stories About Vaginal Birth After Cesarean (VBAC)

Within my very first day of posting comments about VBAC birth videos on YouTube.com, I received an invitation from a pro-VBAC

78

organization, asking me to speak to their members in California. Unfortunately, I had to turn them down (I didn't have time to travel to California that month), but YouTube is extremely popular and it's a great site to promote your book, provided you truly do participate in the community, and don't just spam them.

Believe me, you can find videos on just about any topic in the world on YouTube. Even fiction authors can find videos to comment on while including a one- or two-line signature about their book.

Is your book about business? Do you have any idea how many business presentations appear on YouTube?!

Is your book about origami? There are numerous how-to videos on YouTube showing people folding everything from paper hearts to a life-sized origami crane.

How about a book about digestive disorders? There are even videos about babies passing gas. I'm not kidding! Just type the words *baby* and *fart* into the YouTube search box to see what I mean. You could watch those, and post a humorous comment while including your book's title in your signature.

Are you a horror author? There are videos on YouTube of haunted houses and scary pranks. (Warning—some of them are just downright mean and/or very disturbing to watch.)

Are you a romance author? There are videos on YouTube of romantic surprises couples have staged for each other.

Is your book about babies? There are more cute baby videos on YouTube than you will ever have time to watch. When I need a lift, I type "laughing baby" into YouTube's search box. They are adorable!

NOTE: You can see how popular a video is by looking at the number of views. The more views there are, the most likely your comment will be seen by future viewers because those videos have gone "viral."

___ Day 50 +

Go to:
https://www.youtube.com/

Use some of the keywords on your Book Marketing Cheat Sheet to start finding YouTube videos you can comment on. This is one of the more enjoyable exercises in this book, so have fun!

Posting Your Own YouTube Videos

Not only can you promote your book in the comments boxes on YouTube, but you can also set up your own profile page, and post your own videos or book trailers.

You can see numerous book trailer videos we have created for BookLocker authors here:
https://www.youtube.com/channel/UCMpGLCXsemSu774eYLVmuGg

To see how two authors have created their own YouTube promotional pages, visit the following links:

Dr. Stephen Grinstead is the author of *Thank You Adversity For Yet Another Test: A Body Mind Spirit Approach For Relieving Chronic Pain Suffering.* His YouTube profile page is here:
https://www.youtube.com/user/drstevegrinstead

Wilhelmina McKittrick is the author of *Self-Awareness - Re-Discovering Your Truth* and *Moradyga - A Place Beyond Time.* Her YouTube profile page is here:
https://www.youtube.com/user/Wilhelminamckittrick

Posting Your Book Trailer on YouTube

Perhaps you don't have time to create an entire series of videos for YouTube. Not to worry. You can still post videos on the site to promote your book(s).

A Book Trailer is a short video that draws potential readers in, hopefully making the book irresistible. Think of it as a commercial for your book, but one that's inexpensive to produce. Check out our book trailer service here:
https://marketplace.writersweekly.com/trailer/

___ Day 51 +

Go to http://www.youtube.com.

Click Log In and then Sign Up.

Once you've signed up, get to work setting up your personal profile. Don't be shy about adding information about your website, newsletter, and books. Come up with a list of video ideas you can create from your own home office. How about doing a reading of one of your chapters? Perhaps pull up some of your old articles and turn them into how-to videos? And, don't forget to offer book trailers!

+ These are ongoing activities. Please refer to "AFTER 90 DAYS: YOUR BOOK'S DAILY MARKETING PLAN" near the end of this book.

Days 52–56:

Comment Marketing on Blogs

A blog is basically a regularly-updated website with posts appearing in dated format, from newest to oldest. Almost all of them allow comments under their posts. This chapter might seem long but we have tons of real estate to cover when promoting our books through comment boxes under blog posts!

Finding blogs is very easy. At the very end of most blogs, you can find a box where you can instantly post a comment. Some require you to log in, but many allow anonymous posts, meaning you don't have to create an account to post a comment, or wait to have your account approved. Some blogs are moderated. If your comment doesn't appear instantly, it will after the blog owner approves it.

I've sold hundreds of copies of my book, *DON'T CUT ME AGAIN! True Stories About Vaginal Birth After Cesarean (VBAC),* by simply posting comments to blogs that are discussing VBACs.

When I find a blog post that might be attracting my book's target audience (pregnant women who have previously had a cesarean), I read the post, and then post my own comment. I don't do any hard selling at all as doing so may be considered spam. I give my opinions and experiences (and I really enjoy doing that!) and then I sign my name like this:

Angela Hoy
Author, *DON'T CUT ME AGAIN! True Stories About Vaginal Birth After Cesarean (VBAC)*

You can, of course, start your own blog at a variety of sites. But, you already have your own website and ezine to maintain and publish so I wouldn't recommend setting up shop on these sites just to republish what you've already published on your own. I've found it's less labor-intensive, and more effective, to simply comment on other people's existing blogs where you can take advantage of preexisting audiences instead of needing to build your own from scratch all over again.

You can find a list of popular blogs here: https://detailed.com/50/

That site is updated every 24 hours.

___ Day 52 +

Go to the site above, and click on the first link. Search that site for keywords appearing in your Book Marketing Cheat Sheet. If you can sort the blog posts by date, do that. Click on the most recent one, read the blog post, and then post an informative or opinion comment underneath the post. Be sure to put your signature under the text of your post to promote your website and/or book(s).

If you don't find anything, move on to the next blog on the list.

___ Day 53 +

Repeat the actions from Day 52 while continuing on down the list of the most popular blogs.

___ Day 54 +

Repeat what you did yesterday. It's going to take you awhile to get through the 50 most popular blogs, along with posts that might be attracting your potential readers.

BLOG SEARCH ENGINE

A well-known blog search engine is: http://www.blogsearchengine.org

Use the site's search box to look for the keywords and phrases in your Book Marketing Cheat Sheet. Note that some of the sites that pop up won't be actual blogs. Skip those.

___ Day 55 +

Open your Book Marketing Cheat Sheet and once again pull up your top five keywords or phrases. Now, go to the site above, and search for your top keyword or phrase. Find at least five blog posts that you may want to comment on (preferably more). Read the posts, and then post your own comments while subtly promoting your book by only using your name, the word *Author*, and your book title as your signature, like mine appears earlier in this chapter.

You can do this with your other lists of keywords as well.

WANT MORE?

If you have way too much time on your hands, use your favorite search engine to find even more blogs.

___ Day 56 +

With your Book Marketing Cheat Sheet in hand, go to Google.com or your favorite search engine, and search for your first keyword or phrase and the word blog (no quotes). Choose the top five or ten. Read some posts, and then post comments using your subtle signature (Name, Author and Book Title only).

You can do this with your other lists of keywords as well.

+ These are ongoing activities. Please refer to "AFTER 90 DAYS: YOUR BOOK'S DAILY MARKETING PLAN" near the end of this book.

Days 57:

The Most Popular News Site Blogs on the Internet

by Angela Hoy

Did you know that many popular news sites use a blogging format for their posts? And, yes, most of them allow comments under their posts!

___ Day 57 +

Go to:
https://www.lifewire.com/top-most-popular-blogs-3486365

Click on the most popular news blog. Then, use the search box to look for posts related to your book's topic, or ones that might be of interest to your potential readers. Perform comment marketing under those posts using your subtle signature.

+ This is an ongoing activity. Please refer to "AFTER 90 DAYS: YOUR BOOK'S DAILY MARKETING PLAN" near the end of this book.

Days 58–61:

Posting Comments to National News Websites

by Angela Hoy

When a story is posted to a national news site, you will often find a ripple effect of posts to other news sites, and to blogs as well. This often happens with stories put out by major news syndicates, such as The Associated Press. If a national news story hits really close to home with your book's topic, you have a great chance to share your opinions with millions of people, and to subtly spread the word about your book. But, you need to act fast.

A news story appeared on a major news site about a woman who was given a c-section when she wasn't even pregnant. The woman was suffering from pseudocyesis (false pregnancy) and was "in labor" in the hospital for two days before doctors decided to operate. You would assume the fetal heart rate monitor, which, of course, didn't register a fetal heart rate, or the typical blood work done on laboring women, or the physical exams she undoubtedly had would have all been keys to her diagnosis. But they operated regardless, after treating her for two whole days.

As you can imagine, this article incited rage in readers and people started posting comments and links to it on their blogs, and on other news sites. I posted a comment about the greed of doctors and hospitals, how they make far more on c-sections than vaginal births, and how they're only too happy to cut a woman open rather than let nature take its course. Of course, I included the word *Author* and the title of my book under my name. After posting that to the national news site, I searched https://news.google.com for a couple of exact phrases from that article, and found numerous other websites that were discussing the story as well. Many of them allowed readers to comment so I was able to participate in those discussions, too, while subtly promoting my book in my two-line signature.

Below are some of the major news sites that allow readers to post comments. Note: Some of them may require you to sign up for a free account.

When going to each site, first read through the headlines to see whether there's anything related to your book, or even just a story you feel compelled to comment on. Even if it isn't related to your book, you can still post your opinion under the story, and include your subtle signature.

Note: Some news sites allow comments under some articles, but not under others. Some also stop accepting new comments under articles after a specific period of time has passed, or if the comments get too heated.

As of this writing, CNN, CBS News, MSNBC, and USA Today no longer allows comments under their articles.

___ Day 58 +

ABC News
https://abcnews.go.com

At the news site above, read recent news stories, and/or search for topic-specific stories related to your website, ezine, and/or book(s). Post comments under the stories while subtly promoting your book under your signature. If the site allows you to sort the search results by date, it's best to post under newer articles.

___ Day 59 +

Repeat the instructions above on this site.

Fox News
https://www.foxnews.com

___ Day 60 +

Repeat the instructions above on this site:

Wall Street Journal

http://www.WSJ.com (No, they don't just cover financial news!)

The Wall Street Journal allows you to only view a very small number of articles over a period of time so be very picky about which ones you click on. Only choose the ones that you know people interested in reading might be reading.

___ Day 61 +

Find more popular news sites here:
http://www.ebizmba.com/articles/news-websites

Not all of those sites allow comment posting, but some do.

+ This is an ongoing activity. Please refer to "AFTER 90 DAYS: YOUR BOOK'S DAILY MARKETING PLAN" near the end of this book. New articles are published every single day. Stay on top of them and you'll continue to sell books.

Days 62–66:

Posting Comments to Localized Major News Sites

Many "local" newspapers attract a nationwide and even worldwide audience to their websites. We're going to promote our books on their sites, too, just as we did in the previous chapter.

Here's the catch. Many newspaper websites no longer allow comments. Still others, with the advertising sales way down, charge people to read more than one, or two, or a few articles per month. Below, we've listed the seven most popular ones that, as of this writing, still allow comments on their websites.

As you did before, when going to each site, first read through the headlines to see whether there's anything related to your book, or even just a story you feel compelled to comment on. Even if it isn't related to your book, you can still post your opinion under the story, and then include your subtle signature.

Again, some news sites allow comments under some articles, but not under others. Some also stop accepting new comments under articles after a specific period of time has passed, or when the comments become too heated.

As of this writing, the following major local news sites no longer allow comments:
LATimes.com
NYDailyNews.com
NYPost.com
ChicagoTribune.com
NewsDay.com (their site says the comments are currently on hold)

___ Day 62 +

New York Times
https://www.nytimes.com

At the news site above, read recent news stories, and/or search for topic-specific stories related to your website, ezine, and/or book(s). Post comments under the stories while using your subtle signature.

___ Day 63 +

Repeat the instructions above on this website:

The Washington Post
https://www.washingtonpost.com/

___ Day 64 +

Repeat the instructions above on this website:

New York Post
https://nypost.com/

___ Day 65 +

Repeat the instructions above on these websites:

San Jose Mercury News / Contra Costa Times / The Oakland Tribune
https://www.mercurynews.com/

Houston Chronicle
https://www.chron.com/

___ Day 66 +

Repeat the instructions above on these websites:

Philadelphia Inquirer / Daily News
https://www.inquirer.com
Denver Post
https://www.denverpost.com/

MORE
You can find a list of the nation's 100 largest newspapers right here:
http://nyjobsource.com/papers.html

Remember, not all of them allow comments. If you find one that doesn't, simply move on to the next one on the list.

+ This is an ongoing activity. Please refer to "AFTER 90 DAYS: YOUR BOOK'S DAILY MARKETING PLAN" near the end of this book. New stories are being posted all day, every single day, on localized and national news sites. Stay on top of them and you'll continue to sell books. Return to this chapter, daily if you want, in your ongoing book marketing efforts.

Days 67–70:

News Search Engines

The top news search engines feature links to news stories online as well as some of their own original content. You can find news stories related to the topic of your book, or stories you just want to comment about, while including the title of your book in your signature (your subtle signature).

___ Day 67 +

Google
https://news.google.com

Review the headlines or use their search box to find stories related to the keywords appearing in your Book Marketing Cheat Sheet. Post comments under those stories while subtly promoting your book(s) under your signature.

___ Day 68 +

Follow the instructions above for these sites:

Yahoo
https://news.yahoo.com

AOL
https://www.aol.com

___ Day 69 +

Follow the instructions above for these sites:

Digg
https://digg.com

Feedly
https://feedly.com

We highly recommend reading <u>this tutorial</u> if you aren't familiar with Feedly.

___ Day 70 +

Follow the instructions above for other news aggregator sites. You can find those here:

https://www.wpbeginner.com/showcase/best-news-aggregator-websites-how-to-build-your-own/

+ This is an ongoing activity. Please refer to "AFTER 90 DAYS: YOUR BOOK'S DAILY MARKETING PLAN" near the end of this book. New stories are being posted all day, every single day, on major news search engines. Stay on top of them and you'll continue to sell books. Return to this chapter, daily if you want, in your ongoing book marketing efforts.

Days 71–72:

News Magazines

Like national news sources, news magazines are extremely popular and accessible worldwide via the Internet. You can access a seemingly infinite number of news and human interest stories on these sites, where you can then post comments concerning the topic of your book, or comments about any topic while subtly promoting your book under your signature. All the major news magazines below allow posting of comments by readers.

As of this writing, the following major news magazine websites no longer allow comments:
Time.com
USNews.com
TheEconomist
Wired.com
TheAtlantic.com
Fortune.com
RD.com (Reader's Digest)
TheWeek.com

___ Day 71 +

Review the headlines at the sites below, or use their search box to find stories related to your book or the keywords appearing in your Book Marketing Cheat Sheet. Post comments under those stories while subtly promoting your website, newsletter, and/or book(s) under your signature.

Newsweek
https://www.newsweek.com

___ Day 72 +

Follow the instructions above on these sites:

https://parade.com
https://www.saturdayeveningpost.com

MORE
You can find more news magazines here:
https://www.alexa.com/topsites/category/Top/News/Magazines_and_
E-zines

Remember that not all of them allow comment posting.

ONGOING
+ This is an ongoing activity. Please refer to "AFTER 90 DAYS: YOUR BOOK'S DAILY MARKETING PLAN" near the end of this book. New news stories are being posted each day on national news magazine websites. Stay on top of them and you'll continue to sell books. Return to this chapter, daily if you want, in your ongoing book marketing efforts.

Day 73:

The Most Popular Websites on the Internet

Now that you're adept at finding articles, blogs, discussion lists, and more to promote your book, you can strike out on your own by researching the most popular websites online.

___ Day 73 +

Go here: https://www.alexa.com/topsites

On that page, you can view a list of the most popular websites on the Internet (many were mentioned previously in this book) and you can also view by country or category.

This will probably take more than a day. Surf to the most popular websites you haven't yet visited in your marketing activities, and make a list of the ones you'd like to return to for future promotional activities, like offering excerpts, posting comments, and other promotional tasks listed in this book. Add your list of promising websites to your Book Marketing Cheat Sheet, and include them in your future marketing activities.

ONGOING
+ This is an ongoing activity. Please refer to "AFTER 90 DAYS: YOUR BOOK'S DAILY MARKETING PLAN" near the end of this book.

Days 74–75:

Promoting and/or Selling Your Book on EBAY

by Angela Hoy

eBay can be not only a lucrative site on which to sell your book(s) but it can also be used to *promote* your website and ezine/blog/book(s). How? Well, you have to be a bit clever but it can be done.

Here's my eBay success story.

My Ebook on eBay
217 Copies x $14.95 = $3244.15
(over a two-year period)

I'd read about authors selling their books on eBay over the years. However, I was naturally skeptical. With all the books available on that site, what are the chances a buyer will find my book, and buy it? Under which category do I post it? How does it work? How much does eBay charge? How could I possibly make a profit from doing this?

One rainy Saturday, I was surfing eBay, looking at dolls (I'm a doll collector) and I decided, since it was dreary outside and we weren't going anywhere, perhaps I'd register as an eBay seller, and see how things worked. Instead of listing one of my print books, I decided to list one of my ebooks, *How to Reborn a Doll in a Day* (https://booklocker.com/books/1670.html). I figured I'd pay a few bucks, list it, and just see what would happen.

Lucky for me, there is an entire community of reborn doll enthusiasts online—both artists and buyers—and many of them hang out on eBay. As a newbie, it took me about 45 minutes to find my way through the sign-up and listing process, and to place my first ad. I splurged, buying an ad for a "featured item." Then I posted some photos and a lengthy description, complete with the table of contents, and more. The ad cost me $28.06. I listed several copies for sale under the "Buy It Now" option so people wouldn't have to bid on my ebooks, and could receive them the same day. I gave them information for my Paypal account so eBay could deposit my money there.

I listed the book for $14.95, which is $2.00 more than I sell it for on BookLocker.com. I made the price higher to help pay for the eBay ad costs, and the PayPal transaction fees.

I placed the ad under the Reborn category, where they sell dolls, doll parts, other supplies, and how-to information. Then, I waited. I placed the ad on January 13th. I sold my first book on January 15th. Then I sold another, and another, and another. I was selling a couple of books a day, and making quite a profit! I'd notice a spike in sales just after I'd list a 10-day ad, and another spike just before each ad expired. Sometimes, I sold up to five copies a day. (Ads that are new or about to expire usually pop up at the top of an eBay visitor's computer screen, depending on how they have their viewing preferences set.) We made several hundred dollars in just a couple of months. Whenever an ad would expire, I'd just put it back on eBay with one click and the orders would continue. I experimented with cheaper ads that ran more frequently, but none paid off more than the Featured Item ads.

After three months of basking in the gravy that particular ad was generating (86 copies in the first three months), I was stunned when I received a naughty email from eBay saying they'd received a complaint from another eBay member, claiming my book was in the wrong category. What? I had 100% positive feedback from buyers praising my book on eBay! I was selling copies almost every single day! How could it be in the wrong category? Didn't eBay look at this information before pulling my ad? It didn't take long to figure out what happened.

I'd received a few complaint emails from reborn artists over the months, claiming I couldn't teach someone how to do what they did in just one day. These became especially harsh after my book was featured favorably in *Doll Crafter Magazine*. However, I'd anticipated a backlash from the reborn artists when first writing the book, and I had included a note in the introduction that stated, "I'm sure many reborn artists will be a bit perturbed by the information I'm going to share with you in this book. I only ask that they understand that most of us can't afford to pay hundreds of dollars for a professional reborn doll, but we'd love to have one in our collection (or give one to a loved one) if we can do it inexpensively on our own!"

So, I was pretty sure an artist was angry that I was advertising a book about their craft where they were selling their expensive dolls, and had turned me in. No bother. I sent emails back and forth with eBay and they gave me another category where they suggested I place the ad. It was under Dolls & Bears—Dolls—Artist Offerings—OOAK, Reborn—Other.

I listed the ad under that category. Not surprisingly, sales slowed to a trickle. Instead of selling a couple of books a day, I was down to selling about 4 books a week. While disappointing, it was still gravy and I'd definitely recommend other authors try this method as well. Just be sure to list your book under your book's topic on eBay, not under "books." If your book is a how-to, so much the better!

One thing I noticed after placing my ebook on eBay was that sales of the book increased on BookLocker.com as well. Here's why. I had specifically asked the cover artist to put my website URL, AngelaHoy.com, in a very large font on the front cover of the book. People could easily read that on the cover thumbnail appearing on eBay and they would then go to my website. The link to buy the book at my site, of course, took them to BookLocker.com. It's a good idea to make your URLs visible online on those small cover graphics (thumbnails) featured on eBay, Amazon, and many other sites. This simple ploy was so successful that I've done the same thing on three other book covers since then, including this book.

You can read another non-fiction book eBay success story here:
https://writersweekly.com/success-stories/my-ebay-publishing-success-story-by-matthew-sparks

Okay, admittedly, selling an ebook on eBay works best for non-fiction books. However, if you have a pile of fiction books you want to sell at a reduced rate, why not use eBay for that while also using it to promote your website and/or ezine/blog like I did with my book cover? eBay.com does have categories for fiction books as well and you can mention on eBay that the book is priced less there than on other sites. Another plus of being an eBay member is that you can participate in their discussion groups and you can use your subtle signature for promotion at the same time.

Even if your book is fiction, you can still try listing it in other categories that relate to your story. For example, if your novel mentions sports, you can list your book under "Sports Mem, Cards & Fan Shop." If your novel is a beach book, you could list it under "Travel." eBay has many categories and subcategories to choose from.

___ Day 74

Go to: https://www.ebay.com

Click on the "Sign In or register" link, which is currently on the top, left-hand side of their homepage. The site is pretty easy to navigate. If you want to list an item to sell, click the Sell button that appears at the top of each page.

___ Day 75

Start participating in eBay's lively discussions online. There are discussions about all their categories. At the top of any eBay page, click Community and then Discussion Boards, Groups, or Chat Rooms.

Click here: https://community.ebay.com

Day 76:

Listing Your Ebook for Sale on BookLocker.com and Other Online Ebook Retailers

This activity will work only if you own the electronic rights to your book. If your book was traditionally published, you most likely do not. However, if your publisher did not publish the ebook edition, and does not own electronic rights (check your contract), you should be able to do this.

If your book is not yet published, please consider using BookLocker.com as your publisher. We'd love to take a look at your manuscript!

If you self-published your book and you don't own the electronic rights to your book, you chose a really greedy publisher. Never give away rights to a company that's using *your* money to publish *your* book!

If you own electronic rights to your book, you can list the PDF version of your ebook at BookLocker.com for free, and you don't need an ISBN to do it.

___ Day 76

Go to: https://secure.booklocker.com/authors/new/form.php

BookLocker.com (owned by the authors of this book) lists and sells PDF versions of ebooks for free, even if they didn't print the book for you. Royalties for PDF versions of ebooks sold directly through BookLocker.com are 70% of the list price for ebooks priced $8.95 or higher and 50% of the list price for ebooks priced under $8.95. BookLocker pays royalties monthly on accounts with a balance of $40 or more.

BookLocker.com is selective about what it sells so you must submit your manuscript for consideration first.

Selling Your eBook on the Kindle, Nook, iPad, iPhone, iPod, and more

BookLocker.com also offers a fee-based service to convert your ebook to ePub and Mobi formats (one price covers both conversions), and to list your ebook on Amazon (for the Kindle), BarnesandNoble.com (for the Nook), Apple (for the iPad, iPod, and iPhone), Kobo (Canada's popular ebook retailer, and Overdrive (which sells ebooks to thousands of schools and libraries worldwide).

Prices for the conversions start at $199, and are extremely competitive.

Days 77–81:

Press Releases Are Boring—News Is Not

by Angela Hoy

Journalists and periodical editors receive countless press releases by email, fax, and mail. Although at WritersWeekly.com don't publish press releases, and never have, we are still inundated with them on a daily basis for everything ranging from publishing services to insurance for the self-employed. But we get far more "new book" press releases than anything else. Let me tell you, even though I'm an avid book reader, it is very rare that I receive a new book press release that keeps me interested past the first sentence. Heck, just reading "For Immediate Release" turns me off and many other journalists feel the same way.

If you don't want your "news" instantly tossed by the vast majority of recipients, never, ever use the phrase "for immediate release."

The biggest mistake you can make when promoting a new book is to put "New Book" or "Just Released" or some other similar, boring statement in the title of your new book press release. Since the proliferation of self-publishing companies. More than a million books are published each year now so having a new book just isn't "news" anymore.

What you absolutely *must* do to get the press and the public interested is to turn your press release into a news story—a *real* news story—and news stories, good ones anyway, don't simply announce new books that have come on the market. They make the book or the author *today's news*.

Let's use a real book as an example. BookLocker.com author Melanie Bowden is the author of *Why Didn't Anyone Tell Me? True Stories of New Motherhood* (https://booklocker.com/books/2639.html). Her book includes stories from women whose post-partum experiences were far

104

from ideal. Rather than distributing a press release that just mentions her new book is available, she could, instead, create a news story based on recent headlines involving post-partum depression or post-partum psychosis.

She doesn't need to rely on the headlines to get attention, however. Melanie could make her own news story, and use any or several of the women in her book as subjects for that news story. From colic, to unexpected c-sections, to breastfeeding problems, Melanie could create a variety of subtle press releases (while not calling them press releases) by writing actual news stories about one or more of the women who appear in her book. These feature articles would be of interest to publications serving women and parents.

When you write an "article" that is, in essence, promoting your book, it is a press release. When you make that press release a news article, the press is much more apt to grab your story, and run with it. You've not only given their readers a great story (and only a tiny, subtle marketing blurb), but you've also made a journalist's job much easier that day! They won't need to rewrite what you've written, and may only need to make a few changes, or none at all. What more could a journalist (and a hopeful author) want?

Okay, let's look at another book. *What's Your Anger Type?* (https://booklocker.com/books/2510.html) is a book by Peter Sacco, Ph.D. It teaches people how to learn to identify, control, and modify their anger immediately. He could attempt to get press when violent acts make national headlines, when the perpetrators were, obviously, angry at someone or about something before acting. When you're an expert in a certain area, as Dr. Sacco is, it's not only easy to get press for your new book (provided your press release is a news article), but you might also be added to the journalists' experts databases so they can call on you for future interviews when news stories require that type of expertise.

Jim Croft, author of *The Muslim Masquerade* (https://booklocker.com/books/1316.html), probably will never run out of news story ideas to promote his book. Terrorism and/or the Middle East is in the news almost daily.

When releasing a new novel, you can almost always think of a newsy slant, not only about the book, but also about you, the author.

Coming up with hooks like these is actually fun! If you're having a hard time finding a newsy slant to your book or about yourself, ask people who have read your book if they have any ideas. And of course, don't discount your fellow writers! I can imagine a flurry of creativity if an author were seeking this type of help on the the online writing forums!

Always remember: Press releases are boring. News is not.

___ Day 77

Come up with five to ten different news story ideas to promote your book.

___ Day 78

Choose the story idea you think is most likely to be picked up by the media. Enlist the opinions of other writers online if you wish. You can find the most popular online writing communities here: https://blog.reedsy.com/writing-community

Write and edit your news story. Don't forget to include a short bio at the end (just like a real feature article), mentioning your website, ezine and/or book.

___ Day 79

Read your article once more with a fresh mind, and do a final edit. Get some feedback from other writers on your story before distributing it.

___ Day 80

Distribute your "news story" via these free press release services:

PRLog
https://www.prlog.org/submit-free-press-release.html

PR.com
https://www.pr.com/promote-your-business

PRLog
https://www.prlog.org/

Google "free press release distribution" to find more.

___ Day 81

Submit your news story to ten websites/ezines that you think might run it. Refer back to these two chapters: Days 71–72 and Day 73

Consider spending some money to distribute your news story through one of these professional press release distribution services:

https://www.ereleases.com

https://www.prnewswire.com/

The Guardian publishes book news so definitely contact them!
https://www.theguardian.com/books/booksblog

Days 82–84: Pitch Yourself as an "Expert" or "Source" to News Services and Syndicated Columnists

Non-Fiction Authors

Most good non-fiction authors are considered experts on their book's topic. "Experts" and other authors can be a great interview source for journalists. For example, I have been invited to participate in interviews for stories about Vaginal Birth After Cesarean (VBACs), not because I'm a doctor or midwife, which of course I'm not, but simply because I researched, wrote, and published *DON'T CUT ME AGAIN! True Stories About Vaginal Birth After Cesarean (VBAC).* I've been interviewed by journalists who were writing stories about divorce for different publications because they read about my divorce book. I've also been interviewed by numerous journalists over the years for stories relating to the publishing industry as a direct result of my books for freelance writers and book authors, as well as the popularity of our websites.

Journalists are always looking for an expert or an intriguing person to interview for their current assignment. Why shouldn't *you* be that expert and why shouldn't you get publicity for your book in exchange for your interview time? Put your name out there, and make yourself available for expert interviews by everyone from journalists at major media outlets to freelancers writing for obscure websites. The more you get your name out there, the more you'll be recognized as "the expert" in your field.

You might also notice, after doing a few interviews, that reporters start to contact you for their own stories after seeing you in someone else's. I was featured on NPR several years ago and journalists still contact me with interview requests after listening to that interview. I have also been contacted by reporters who have read about us in the Wall Street Journal. In fact, the Wall Street Journal recently contacted me for an interview on a news story on the publishing industry. The reporter remembered me from another interview several years ago. When he called, he said, "You know more about how Amazon works than most of their employees do."

Publicity definitely has a trickle-down effect. Take advantage of it!

Fiction AND Non-Fiction Authors

You don't have to be a non-fiction author to be considered an expert on one or more topics. Whether your book is fiction or non-fiction, your areas of expertise don't necessarily have to relate to your book to get publicity for that book.

On the flip side, you might be considered an expert on one or more topics specifically because of your novel. Perhaps you did extensive research into a specific geographic area for your romance novel, or researched historical figures who lived in the Fifteenth Century for your historical novel, or spent months studying the tactics of scam artists for your thriller, or examined a specific area of forensics for your detective novel. I could go on and on but, by now, you can see where I'm going with this. Anybody can be an expert about something.

Your expert status doesn't necessarily need to relate to your novel to have your book mentioned in the press. A romance novelist and mother of five could be considered an expert source for articles targeting work-at-home moms, or an expert on self-publishing (if she has successfully self-published), or an expert on belly dancing (if that is her hobby). You don't need to be interviewed on a topic specifically dealing with your book to get your book mentioned.

Any article that features you should also mention your website and/or your book. That's the least the reporter can do to thank you for your time, right? And, you should always ask them to include the name of your book in their article. Don't be shy! You'd be surprised how many authors assume the reporter will do this, only to discover no mention of their book at all in the final article. One author, who was a guest on a national morning news show, learned later they edited out her comments about her book, along with the cover graphic they promised to air. Readers may be so inspired by your "lunchbox assembly line" invention or your "potty-train your toddler in two days" secret that they will want to visit your website, learn more about you, and be so inspired by your ability to write a novel while being a full-time mom that they'll want to buy your book.

Readers want to learn more about their favorite authors, and about new authors whose books they're considering buying. Introduce yourself to new readers through the press by participating in interviews, and then invite them to your website. Be sure to include personal information on your website to satisfy their curiosity about you.

There used to be large directories and databases of experts online but the good ones now cost a lot of money to join. However, this shouldn't stop you from contacting journalists who cover your topic's/genre's "beat" on a regular basis, and offering yourself as a source for their future articles.

What you need to do is find those reporters.

You can search the major news sites and newspapers listed in earlier chapters or you can go a different route, like to a news service. News services, or news syndicates, distribute stories to multiple publications, meaning they syndicate their content. If you get a mention in a news service article, you could find yourself in newspapers nationwide!

For my VBAC "expert status," I went to The Associated Press (https://www.ap.org/en-us), and searched for the word VBAC in their archives. Two articles popped up and they were both written by the same reporter, meaning he's probably the go-to guy for those types of articles. I then found his contact information by Googling his name along with "Associated Press."

More articles popped up and I learned I was right. He's an Associated Press Medical Writer. It took me about 10 seconds to find his blog. Bingo!

I would send him an email that went something like this:

Dear Mike,

I read your two articles, "Caesarean Births Rapidly Rising" and "C-sections in the U.S. Are at an All-Time High." If/when you write articles on VBACs in the future, I'd be very happy to help if you need a source. I was so shocked by my doctor's dishonesty about VBACs during my fifth pregnancy that I fired him, and found another doctor in the next town who was very happy to work with me. I not only had a successful VBAC, but I also interviewed numerous women like myself and published the book, DON'T CUT ME AGAIN! Real Stories of Vaginal Birth After Cesarean.

So if you need an interview source or even a unique story idea, I'd love to help.

Have a beautiful day!

Angela Hoy
Author
https://booklocker.com/books/2845.html

Of course, if you have a truly unique story idea for that reporter, by all means, pitch that idea! Why not be the main topic of one of his or her future feature articles? Journalists are always looking for new and unique story ideas.

Let's do one more and then you'll have a pretty good idea about how to offer yourself up as an "expert" or interview source.

I surfed over to Reuters (https://www.reuters.com), and searched for VBAC. Only one result popped up, so then I searched for "vaginal birth after cesarean." (Ya gotta get creative sometimes to find what you're looking for!) Bingo! Tons of stories popped up. Some of these stories are from other publications that syndicate their stories to more publications, but I did find two reporters working for Reuters Health. I poked around a bit, and found a form on their site where you can submit comments to their editors. I sent an email like the one above to

Reuters Health editors using their online form, while also trying to find the direct contact information for their health reporters.

Bonus! While surfing both associatedpress.com and reuters.com, I was taken to numerous articles and blogs that allowed the immediate posting of comments. If I wasn't so busy writing this book, I'd be on those sites right now, subtly promoting one or more of my books!

___ Day 82

Using our examples above, search for news services and syndicate journalists and columnists at the sites below who might be interested in using you as a source for a future story.

Associated Press
https://www.ap.org/en-us

You can also look at main topics on their website here:
https://www.ap.org/en-us/topics

Creators Syndicate
https://www.creators.com/

nytLicensing
https://nytlicensing.com/search/

___ Day 83

Repeat the step above on this site:

Reuters
https://www.reuters.com

Find more syndicates to search here:
https://www.manta.com/mb_34_A417F_000/news_syndicates

___ Day 84

There are even more news services targeting specific industries, as well as news services that serve other countries. To find these, search https://www.google.com for "news service" along with some of your book's main keywords or phrases.

Day 85:

Directories of Experts

You might not have much luck finding an industry directory that you qualify to join, but you'll never know until you try.

Two examples of industry-specific directories of experts:

Request a Woman in Science
https://500womenscientists.org/request-a-scientist/

Directory of Marine and Freshwater Professionals:
https://www.oceanexpert.net

As you can see, these directories can be on very niche topics!

___ Day 85

See whether you can find a directory of experts in your genre, or for your book's topic(s), by searching your favorite search engine for Experts [your genre/topic].

There are also numerous fee-based directories you can be listed in but they can be very expensive.

This site charges $5 per month to be listed as an expert that journalists can contact:
https://expertisefinder.com/become-an-expert/

Also, check out this list:
https://gijn.org/2016/05/23/resources-guides-to-finding-expert-sources/

Experts.com: $450/year (ouch!)
https://www.experts.com/memberinfo
"The premier registry of Experts on the Internet. It is the oldest and most established expert directory of its kind."

Day 86:

Be the Dear Abby of Your Area of Expertise

by Angela Hoy

People love Q&A columns! Having a Q&A section on your website and/or ezine/blog is an excellent way to attract new readers.

There are lots of places online where you can register to answer people's questions about a specific topic. However, those places don't pay contributors. You can see a list of these types of sites here:

http://www.libraryspot.com/askanexpert.htm

I recommend publishing your own Q&A column on your website. You then own and control the content and you can do whatever you want with it, including publishing compilations of your Q&A columns in a future book!

Each week, I answer a reader's writing- or publishing-related question in our ezine, and also on our website. You can see examples of these here: https://writersweekly.com/category/ask-the-expert

Notice the column is called "Ask the Expert." People know they're getting advice from someone who is qualified to help. If someone asks a question I can't answer, I never hesitate to turn to a qualified author or publishing colleague for help. Of course, I plug them and their book(s) when they lend me a hand!

Fiction authors can do this, too! Perhaps you can answer questions for other aspiring novelists? Or, you can set up a Q&A section where readers can ask your main characters questions. Of course, your characters would love to answer them and you can include these entertaining exchanges in your newsletter as well.

___ Day 86

Add a Q&A Section to your website and ezine/blog. Start soliciting questions in the next issue of your newsletter, and on your website.

Day 87:

Online Radio Shows

by Angela Hoy

I am not a fan of traditional radio shows as a marketing medium. Potential readers usually need to hear your marketing message several times before they'll buy your book. When you participate in a traditional radio show, they hear it only once (unless you're lucky and it's replayed) and then it's all over. Furthermore, if someone is listening in their car while driving, they can't click their computer instantly to buy your book, or even write down the name of your book unless they're a very dangerous driver.

I've been a guest on traditional radio shows and I can honestly say that, with the exception of National Public Radio (NPR), which was broadcast repeatedly in several countries, my radio interviews generated almost zero sales, and were a complete waste of my time. I solicited feedback from authors when researching an article for WritersWeekly on this topic and they almost overwhelmingly agreed. If you're interested, they appear here:
https://writersweekly.com/letters-to-the-editor/radio-interviews-poor-book-sales-for-authors

However, I have participated in two taped **online** interviews that have generated quite a bit of business. The first, with Tom Antion, was an audio interview created as part of a teleseminar series back in 2000. I still get new subscribers and book buyers from that interview today even though it is not a free broadcast.

The second one I did was on BlogTalkRadio.com with *The Publishing Insiders*. Since the interview is online, it can be heard over and over again for as long as the website keeps the interview archived. Furthermore, it's listed in the Internet search engines, something traditional radio shows can't do unless they are later posted online as well.

So, although I don't recommend spending time and effort trying to land traditional radio interviews (except for NPR) that won't be posted online, I do recommend participating in online national or international radio shows. You probably won't be able to land an interview with all the shows you contact but it's worth a shot to approach them, and offer yourself as an interview subject.

BlogTalkRadio is billed as "the leading social radio network." You can create your own live talk show, which can be heard around the world without the need for special equipment, but you can also contact hosts already using their service to offer yourself as a guest.

WARNING: Never, ever pay money to be featured as a guest on a radio show.

___ Day 87

Go here: https://www.blogtalkradio.com/categories

Click on any of the categories that might fit your book and you'll see recently recorded shows, along with the host of each one. After registering, you can click on the contact button to contact the host, and offer yourself as a future guest. Hint: If the show has multiple ratings, it indicates the show is more popular than a show that has no ratings.

You might also find online radio shows hosted by other services by searching your favorite search engine for *online radio show [keyword describing your book]*.

Be sure to remove the brackets when searching.

Day 88:

Book Blogs

There are some hard-core book junkies out there and many have started their own book blogs. Not only can you pitch your book to them for review but you can also post comments under some of the blog posts while subtly promoting your book.

___ Day 88

Research the book blogs below to see whether they might be interested in reviewing your book. You can also post comments under some of the blog posts.

Bustle Books
https://www.bustle.com/

First Page to Last
https://fromfirstpagetolast.wordpress.com/review-policy/

A Life in Books (rarely reviews self-published books)
https://alifeinbooks.co.uk/

Reedsy
https://reedsy.com/discovery/blog

Many more are featured here:
https://www.scribendi.com/advice/best_book_blogs_2015.en.html

And, search your favorite search engine for "book blog" to find even more.

Day 89:

Connecting with Book Lovers

Goodreads says it best on their site:

"Goodreads is a free website for book lovers. Imagine it as a large library that you can wander through and see everyone's bookshelves, their reviews, and their ratings. You can also post your own reviews and catalog what you have read, are currently reading, and plan to read in the future. Don't stop there—join a discussion group, start a book club, contact an author, and even post your own writing."

___ **Day 89 +**

https://www.goodreads.com/

Get an account at Goodreads.com, and start participating in their community. Remember to be very subtle when mentioning your own book(s).

ONGOING
+ This is an ongoing activity. Please refer to "AFTER 90 DAYS: YOUR BOOK'S DAILY MARKETING PLAN" near the end of this book.

Day 90:

More Ideas

Seth Stevenson, an ad critic for *Slate*, tested a Google service that lets people broadcast their own commercial for as little as $100.

Some authors ask for "donations" while serializing their books online.

Many authors keep track of their marketing activities using Google Alerts.

Research all three of these items.

___ **Day 90**

Watch this video*: How I Ran an Ad on Fox News*

https://www.youtube.com/watch?v=peqnSTBnTVk

Read this: Mindy Klasky Tests 'Reader-Supported Serialized Novel'

https://www.adweek.com/galleycat/mindy-klasky-tests-reader-supported-serialized-novel/30611

Read about, and sign up for, Google Alerts. See

https://writersweekly.com/this-weeks-article/why-google-alerts-are-helpful-by-diane-craver

PART II

"AFTER 90 DAYS"

YOUR BOOK'S DAILY MARKETING PLAN

Below is a recommended schedule for your Ongoing Marketing Activities, which were indicated by the + symbol in this book. These are activities we recommend you continue to do on a regular basis to promote your website, newsletter, and book(s).

One thing's for sure:
If you stop promoting your book, it will stop selling!

DAILY

Each day, perform these activities before moving on to the list on the following page.

___ Using the Bookmarks you've been posting to your Book Marketing Cheat Sheet, return to previous online discussions/posts to see whether anyone has posted comments or questions for you. Be sure to sign up for email alerts on sites that offer that service.

___ If you're blogging on your website, update your blog. Even a short post is better than no post at all. The more consistent you are, the more readers you'll have, and the better your search engine rankings will be.

___ Answer all reader emails and other inquiries the same day they are received or, at the very most, within 24 hours. It's okay to take Sundays off if you want. (We occasionally do.) Most people don't expect a response on Sundays.

YOUR BOOK'S DAILY MARKETING PLAN

Each task below references specific days
appearing in previous chapters.

1st Day of the Month

___ Create fresh content! Post a new article to your website. (Days 1–3)

___ Research new stories on localized major news sites, and post comments. (Days 62–66)

2nd

___ Create and distribute a new issue of your ezine, and/or email your subscribers about your current blog updates. (Days 4–11)

3rd

___ Update your Facebook status, and participate in other Facebook users' pages and groups while subtly promoting your book. (Days 47–49)

___ Update your Twitter status, and respond to other Twitter users' Tweets while subtly promoting your book. (Days 47–49)

___ Post comments to national news sites. (Days 58–61)

4th

___ Consider running a contest/sweepstakes in your ezine to attract new subscribers. Offer a nifty prize to a random subscriber, which will be awarded on a specific date. Run ads for your contest in your ezine, on your website, in your email signature, and even on your Facebook and Twitter pages. See "Building Block Book Marketing" - https://writersweekly.com/this-weeks-article/building-block-book-marketing-by-sharon-elaine

___ Research new stories published on news search engines, and post comments. (Days 67–70)

5th

___ Watch YouTube videos related to your book's topic, and post comments while promoting your book, website, and/or newsletter/ezine. Consider creating your own YouTube videos, like a book trailer. (Days 50–51)

___ Visit Goodreads.com, and actively participate in that community. (Day 89)

6th

___ Post comments to blogs. (Days 52–56)

___ Research new stories published on major news magazines, and post comments. (Days 71–72)

7th

___ Research news posts on the most popular blogs, and post comments. (Day 57)

___ Participate in eBay discussions. (Days 74–75)

8th

___ Create fresh content! Post a new article to your website. (Days 1–3)

___ Research new stories on localized major news sites, and post comments. (Days 62–66)

9th

___ Create and distribute a new issue of your newsletter and/or email your subscribers about your current blog updates. (Days 4–11)

10th

___ Update your Facebook status, and participate in other Facebook users' pages and groups while subtly promoting your book. (Days 47–49)

___ Update your Twitter status, and respond to other Twitter users' Tweets while subtly promoting your book. (Days 47–49)

___ Post comments to national news sites. (Days 58–61)

11th

___ Offer your free excerpt to websites, blogs, and other online publications. (Days 42–46

___ Once again review sites with high Google rankings. They change all the time. (Days 37–41)

12th

___ Research new stories published on news search engines, and post comments. (Days 67–70)

___ Visit Goodreads.com, and actively participate in that community. (Day 89)

13th

___ Post comments to blogs. (Days 52–56)

___ Research new stories published on major news magazines, and post comments. (Days 71–72)

14th

___ Research news posts on the most popular blogs, and post comments. (Day 57)

___ Review the most popular websites online. See whether the list has changed, and post comments under new articles appearing on those sites. (Day 73)

15th

___ Create fresh content! Post a new article to your website. (Days 1–3)

___ Research new stories on localized major news sites, and post comments. (Days 62–66)

___ Look for syndicates or columnists who might need an "expert" for their future articles. (Days 82–84)

16th

___ Create and distribute a new issue of your newsletter and/or email your subscribers about your current blog/website updates. (Days 4–11)

17th

___ Update your Facebook status, and participate in other Facebook users' pages and groups while subtly promoting your book. (Days 47–49)

___ Update your Twitter status, and respond to other Twitter users' Tweets while subtly promoting your book. (Days 47–49)

___ Post comments to national news sites. (Days 58–61)

18th

___ Make a list of new story ideas that you can spin into a "press releases." Write, edit, and distribute the best one. (Days 77–81)

19th

___ Research new stories published on news search engines, and post comments. (Days 67–70)

___ Visit Goodreads.com, and actively participate in that community. (Day 89)

___ Watch YouTube videos related to your book's topic, and post comments while promoting your book, website, and/or newsletter. Consider creating your own YouTube videos, like a book trailer. (Days 50–51)

20th

___ Post comments to blogs. (Days 52–56)

___ Research new stories published on major news magazines, and post comments. (Days 71–72)

21st

___ Research news posts on the most popular blogs, and post comments. (Day 57)

___ Offer your free excerpt to websites, blogs, and other online publications. (Days 42–46)

___ Review the most popular websites online. See whether the list has changed, and post comments under new articles appearing on those sites. (Day 73)

22nd

___ Create fresh content! Post a new article to your website. (Days 1–3)

___ Research new stories on localized major news sites, and post comments. (Days 62–66)

23rd

___ Create and distribute a new issue of your newsletter and/or email your subscribers about your current blog updates. (Days 4–11)

24th

___ Update your Facebook status and participate in other Facebook users' pages and groups while subtly promoting your book. (Days 47–49)

___ Update your Twitter status, and respond to other Twitter users' Tweets while subtly promoting your book. (Days 47–49)

___ Post comments to national news sites. (Days 58–61)

25th

___ Once again review sites with high Google rankings. They change all the time. (Days 37–41)

___ Participate in eBay discussions. (Days 74–75)

26th

___ Visit the major online bookstores to look for new reviews posted about your book(s). If you find some good ones, contact the reviewers to request permission to quote them. Add those to your Book Marketing Cheat Sheet, to your website and newsletter, and post them to your social media accounts. (Day 31)

___ Research new stories published on news search engines, and post comments. (Days 67–70)

27th

___ Post comments to blogs. (Days 52–56)

___ Research new stories published on major news magazines, and post comments. (Days 71–72)

___ Review comments sent in by readers (you should have been posting these to your Book Marketing Cheat Sheet) and consider posting fresh ones on your website, in your newsletter and to your social media accounts. (Day 32)

28th

___ Research news posts on the most popular blogs, and post comments. (Day 57)

___ Consider distributing an old article appearing on your website to the free article websites. (Days 26–30)

29th

___ Read the marketing materials in your Book Marketing Cheat Sheet to see whether anything needs to be updated or freshened up.

___ Look for Amazon affiliate stores that might want to feature your book. (Bonus Marketing Activities in the following chapter.)

30th

___ Visit Goodreads.com, and actively participate in that community. (Day 89)

___ Create new, fresh ads/blurbs for your books to run in your newsletter.

PART III

Bonus Marketing Activities

Finding Amazon.com Affiliate Bookstores

by Richard Hoy

Many websites take advantage of Amazon's affiliate program by listing books for sale on their sites. The URLs they use to send website visitors to Amazon.com contain their affiliate code. When somebody clicks to buy, the website earns affiliate income on the sale.

These websites are usually happy to hear about new books their readers might be interested in, and from which that the website can profit. To find these stores, go to:

Go to: https://www.google.com/advanced_search

In the blank box at the top, next to the "all these words" option, type this (but don't include the parentheses):

"In association with Amazon.com," bookstore, (keyword describing your book).

For example, for Angela's VBAC book, I typed "In association with Amazon.com," bookstore, vbac

The first page that popped up for me was a large, very professional website about home births. The page contained an extensive list of books that target the same audience as Angela's. When we find a page like this, Angela locates the website's contact information on the site, and sends them a short note like this:

Hi there,

I noticed you have a large list of Amazon.com affiliate books on your site.

My book, DON'T CUT ME AGAIN! True Stories About Vaginal Birth After Cesarean (VBAC), is available on Amazon.com here:

https://www.amazon.com/AGAIN-Stories-About-Vaginal-Cesarean/dp/1591139945

I think it might be of interest to your readers and I'd be thrilled if you added my book to your online bookstore.

If you'd like a free excerpt to run on your website, or if you publish a newsletter and would like an excerpt for that, I'd love to send it to you.

Have a beautiful day!

Angela Hoy
Author, DON'T CUT ME AGAIN! True Stories About Vaginal Birth After Cesarean (VBAC)

Not every result will be a bookstore or a site you'll want to deal with but this search will greatly improve your chances of finding appropriate affiliate sites.

A variation on the search would be to substitute, "In association with Amazon.com" in the search string with just "amazon.com."

This strategy is much better than simply asking a bunch of sites to link to your book. You are helping people make more money and improve their bookstores versus asking for a free link. Site owners are more responsive when you help them make money.

Using the keywords or phrases in your Book Marketing Cheat Sheet, and following the steps above, try to find at least 10 online bookstores that might be interested in carrying your book.

Many More Creative Marketing Ideas!

At WritersWeekly.com, we purchase "Marketing Secrets" articles from writers and publishers every week. Many of their ideas are true gems! You can see a list of the articles here:
https://writersweekly.com/marketing-secrets

For hundreds of other articles on online and offline book marketing, as well as other industry tidbits, please visit:

https://writersweekly.com/category/angela-desk

Popular topics include:

How to Sell to Books on Consignment to Bookstores and Other Retailers

Do NOT Sneak Your Self-Published Book onto Bookstore Shelves!

Top Signs a Book is Self-Published

Should Authors Abandon Print Books For Ebooks Only? HECK NO!

10 Reasons NOT to Sell Your Own Book

Print on Demand (POD) Secrets Revealed!

Does Amazon Remove Old Book Listings? No!

DON'T Hire a Designer BEFORE Choosing a Publisher!

How to Remember, Write and Publish Your Life Story

WHO'S SCAMMING GRANNY? Snakes That Prey on Elderly Authors

How I Made $10K Last Month Writing and Selling Erotica by Anonymous

and hundreds more!

About the Authors

Angela Hoy is well-known in the online freelance writing community as the publisher and editor of WritersWeekly.com, a site that publishes new freelance jobs and paying markets every Wednesday. She is also an advocate for writers' rights, publishing numerous articles on how writers can protect themselves from deadbeat editors and publishers as well as common industry scams. She is the author of 25 books, and the co-author of 2 additional books. Her book, *How to Be a Syndicated Newspaper Columnist*, was one of the first ebooks created and sold online.

Richard Hoy is a former Internet marketing executive. He's developed and executed online promotional strategies for Hoechst Marion Roussel (now Aventis Pharmaceuticals, Inc.), DirecTV, and Compaq Computers Medium and Small Business Division, as well as a host of smaller firms. From 1996 to 1999, he was moderator of the Online Advertising Discussion list, the first discussion community on the Internet dedicated to the subject of online advertising. In 1999, Richard created and edited *The ClickZ Guide to Email Marketing,* one of the first compendiums on the subject of the then-emerging field of email marketing. He was a regular speaker at the popular *Web Advertising and Web Marketing* conference series back in the heyday of the dotcom boom. He was also a well-received columnist on ClickZ from 2000 to 2001, where he wrote a column on small business use of the Internet.

Richard "retired" from BookLocker in 2019 (he is still available for consultations and other help, thank goodness) in order to launch BoostaBook.com, which offers creative marketing options for authors, including his extremely popular and extremely affordable *Category and Keyword Analysis* service.

The Hoys reside on Florida's gulf coast.

If you'd like BookLocker.com to consider your manuscript for publication, contact them here: http://publishing.booklocker.com

Index

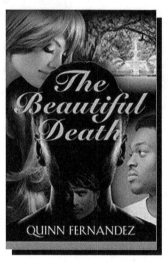

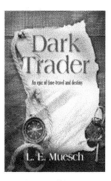

More Unsolicited Testimonials

https://publishing.booklocker.com/testimonials

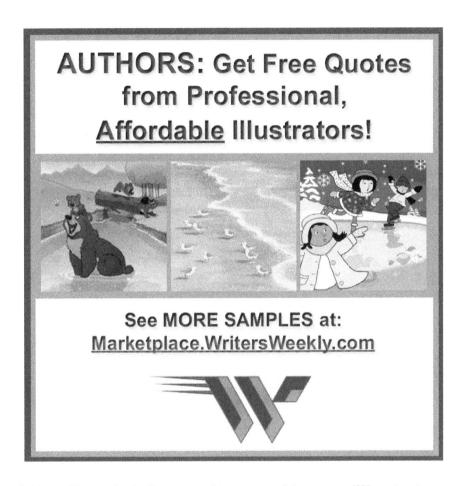